The Cotton Patch Version of Luke and Acts

Jesus' Doings and the Happenings

The Cotton Patch Version of
Luke and Act

Jesus' Doings and the Happenings

CLARENCE JORDAN

Association Press
Follett Publishing Company/Chicago

THE COTTON PATCH VERSION OF LUKE AND ACTS
Jesus' Doings and the Happenings

International Standard Book Number: 0-695-81173-8

Library of Congress Catalog Card Number: 78-19582

456789/8281807978

Printed in the United States of America

Contents

Introduction

The purpose of the "cotton patch" approach to the scriptures is to help the modern reader have the same sense of participation in them which the early Christians must have had. This approach is explained in detail in the first volume of this series—*The Cotton Patch Version of Paul's Epistles*. By stripping away the fancy language, the artificial piety, and the barriers of time and distance, this version puts Jesus and his people in the midst of our modern world, living where we live, talking as we talk, working, hurting, praying, bleeding, dying, conquering, alongside the rest of us. It seeks to restore the original feeling and excitement of the fast-breaking *news*—good news—rather than musty history.

To be sure, this is a risky undertaking. For one thing, it simply can't be done with absolute accuracy. Matching present-day people, groups and settings with their biblical counterparts involves a good bit of guesswork and subjective interpretation, mingled with the best knowledge one has of both the modern and ancient situation. For example, I have paired the Pharisees with church members, and the scribes with theologians and seminary professors. This may pinch, and may well be challenged. In fact, I gladly yield to those who may do a better job of matching. There are times, too, when the circumstances defy the technique of "cotton patching," such as Stephen's long historical speech (Happenings 7:1-53) and Paul's shipwreck (Happenings 27:1-28:15). In these instances we simply return to the original setting. It is hoped—perhaps in vain—that this capricious century-jumping will neither lose nor confuse you.

Another thing which makes this approach risky is that it may make the New Testament characters, particularly Jesus, too contemporary and therefore too human, thus laying oneself open to charges of sacrilege and irreverence. Jesus has been so zealously worshipped, his deity so vehemently affirmed, his halo so brightly illumined, and his cross so beautifully polished that in the minds of many he no longer exists as a man. He has become an exquisite celestial being who momentarily and mistakenly lapsed into a painful involvement in the human scene, and then quite properly returned to his heavenly habitat. By thus glorifying him we more effectively rid ourselves of him than did those who tried to do so by crudely crucifying him.

Obviously this is not the thrust of the Bible. Its emphasis all the way through is on the *humanity* of God—Immanuel, God-with-us; upon incarnation—the word become flesh, here and now, in our own experiences. Its movement is from heaven earthward, not vice versa.

So the "cotton patch" version unashamedly takes the side of human beings rather than the angels. In so doing, it is as offensive as the incarnation, as indecent as the Almighty God dying ignobly as a man on a cross.

But admitting the risks, perhaps the rewards will more than off-set them. Possibly the wind of Pentecost will blow through our houses, and its fire enkindle our hearts. Maybe Jesus, the great interpreter of the scriptures, will join us and enlighten us on our journey from Atlanta to Austell even as he did the two disciples on their way from Jerusalem to Emmaus. He may let us sit at his feet and wash them with our tears. Perhaps he'll startle us with his parables and powerful sermons, and sting us with his honest rebukes. He may come alive. And we too.

In case some of you are wondering why Luke and Acts are tied together, let me point out that they are but two volumes, by the same author, of the biography of Jesus. The first is an account of the life of Christ as one man, Jesus of Nazareth, and comes to a fitting climax with the ascension. As this episode ends the curtain falls, but we are told not to go away; the drama is not over. The second volume, or act two, then picks up the story and describes the life of Christ in his new body, the church. Since this story is not complete, nor will it be until the end of time, it could not be brought to a climax. It merely stops, as though the author is saying, "Here's where I get off; y'all take it from here." Luke-Acts, then, as the first two volumes in the still unfinished biography of Jesus, should never have been separated by the Gospel of John.

Luke the physician, generally believed to be the author of these two volumes, or scrolls, presents his material with tremendous literary skill and artistry. While seeking to preserve this and at the same time simplifying it for my companions of the cotton patch, I have been caught often in the scholar-farmer bind. So the text may seem to be quite polished in one sentence and a bit uncouth in the next. I beg your forbearance, for this bumpiness is a fairly common foible of one who must stand in both camps at once and act as go-between.

No one can be more painfully aware than I of the faults and imperfections of this humble attempt to capture the spirit and meaning of the Lukan writings, and to share them with my contemporaries. But even so, this is the way they have come through to me after immersing myself in the Greek scriptures and in the day-to-day affairs of the human situation. With all the shortcomings, then, I pass them on to you with the fervent hope that you may thereby be encouraged and strengthened in your life in Christ.

Clarence L. Jordan

Koinonia Farm
Americus, Georgia

9

Jesus' Doings
[LUKE]

Jesus' Doings [LUKE]

1.

My dear Friend of God:

A number of people have already undertaken to write a book about the events which have occurred among us, each claiming to be "just as the original eyewitnesses and participants in the cause related them to us." So it seemed wise to me to trace carefully everything from the very beginning and write it down in an orderly fashion, so that you might be *absolutely sure of your information.*

Yours,
Luke

5. In the days when Ole Gene was governor of Georgia, there was a preacher by the name of Zack Harris. His wife was a very aristocratic woman named Elizabeth. They were both strict church members and were careful to observe all the rules and regulations of the Lord. They had no children, since Elizabeth was barren and by now they were both quite old.

8. One day when it was his turn to conduct services (the ministers had worked out a schedule among themselves), Zack went into the study to meditate, while all the people waited prayerfully in the sanctuary for the hour of worship. He looked up and saw a messenger from God standing just to the right of the desk. When Zack Harris saw him, he was quite alarmed and frightened.

13. But the messenger said, "There's no need to be afraid,

Zack Harris, since your prayers have been heard. Your wife Elizabeth will bear you a son, whom you'll call John. He will be your pride and joy, and his birth will bring gladness to many people. He'll be a great man of God. No wine or whiskey will touch his lips, but he'll be full of holy "spirit" while his mother is still carrying him. He'll turn a lot of *church people* toward the Lord their God. God himself will go in front of him with the spirit and power of Elijah. His job will be to turn the hearts of fathers toward their children, and to bring the stubborn around to the thinking of the devoted; in short, to get a dedicated band ready for the Lord."

18. Zack Harris said to the messenger, "How am I to believe all this? You see, I'm an old man, and my wife is well along in years."

19. The messenger replied, "*I* am Gabriel, God's attendant. I was sent to speak to you and to break the good news of these things to you. Now listen, you'll be silent and unable to talk until the day all this happens, because you didn't believe what I told you, which will surely come to pass in due season."

21. Now all this time the people were waiting for Reverend Harris, and they were amazed that he was staying so long in the study. When he did come out, he was unable to speak to them. They recognized that he had had a vision in the study, for he was gesturing to them and remained speechless.

24. When he had wound up his church duties, he went home. Shortly afterwards his wife Elizabeth became pregnant, and for the first five months she didn't go out in public. She was thinking, "The Lord did this for me, to take away the stigma of my sterility."

26. During the sixth month of her pregnancy the messenger Gabriel was sent from God to a city in Georgia by the name of

Valdosta, to a young lady named Mary. She was engaged to a man whose name was Joseph, from one of the old-line families. The messenger went in to her and said, "Hello, you blessed one. THE LORD IS WITH YOU!" She was nearly bowled over by this, and wondered what to make of such a greeting.

30. The messenger said to her, "Don't be so alarmed, Mary, for you have been chosen for a special favor from God. Listen, you'll become pregnant and have a baby boy, whom you'll name Jesus. He'll be a great man, and will be called 'The Almighty's Son.' The Lord God will set him on the throne of his father David, and he'll always be head of the faithful. His movement will never end."

34. Mary said to the messenger, "How can this happen when I'm not even married yet?"

35. The messenger replied, "Holy Spirit will lie upon you, and Power from the Almighty will impregnate you. For this reason the child, sired from on High, will be called 'God's Son.' Now listen, your cousin Elizabeth has also become pregnant with a son, despite her age. And this is now the sixth month for her who was thought to be barren. God will see to it that every word of this will actually happen."

38. So Mary said, "All right then, I am at the Lord's service. I want it to be just as you have said." At that the messenger left her.

39. Soon after this, Mary quickly packed up and went to a town in the hills of north Georgia. She arrived at the home of Zack Harris and greeted Elizabeth. And do you know what happened? When Elizabeth heard Mary's greeting, the baby in her womb gave a kick. And Elizabeth bubbled over with Holy Spirit and shouted as loud as she could, "Praise the Lord for a woman

15

like you! And praise the Lord for your baby! How did a thing like this ever happen to me—the mother of my Lord coming to me? Because listen here, when the sound of your greeting entered my ears, the baby in my womb kicked for joy. It's a wonderful woman who has believed that the words spoken to her from the Lord will become a reality."

And Mary said,
"My soul exalts the Lord
And my heart exults before God my Savior.
For he has disregarded my humble origin,
And from now on the ages will honor me.
Great things the Almighty did for me,
And Holy be his name.
From generation to generation
His mercy showers those who fear him.
With his strong arm
He scatters the big boys
Who think they're somebody.
He pulls thrones from under the royalty
And gives dignity to the lowly.
He loads the hungry with good things
But the rich he lets go with nothing at all.
Mindful of mercy, he gives a lift to his people
Just as he promised our fathers—
Abraham our father and his many descendants."

Mary stayed with her about three months and then returned to her home.

57. Now when Elizabeth's term was up, she gave birth to a boy. The neighbors and her relatives heard that the Lord had been mighty good to her, and they shared her joy. The day came for the child to be christened, and they were calling him by the name of his father, Zack Harris. But his mother said, "No, he'll be called John."

61. They said to her, "But none of your kinfolk is named that." So they made signs to his father to find out what he wanted him to be called.

63. He asked for pencil and paper and wrote, "His name is John."

They were all quite surprised. Then right away Reverend Harris's tongue and mouth started working again, and he was praising God.

65. All the neighbors were simply dumbfounded, and the story of these events was repeated time and again through the hills of north Georgia. People tucked it away in their memories, saying, "What will this child grow up to be? For the hand of God is surely on him."

67. His father bubbled over with Holy Spirit and started preaching,

"Praise the Lord, the God of our nation,
Because he took notice of us, and arranged a way out for his people.
In the house of David his child
He raised up a bugler to sound deliverance for us,
Just as he spoke through the mouth of the holy prophets of old—
'Deliverance from our enemies
And from the hand of all who hate us.'
He did well by our fathers
And honored his solemn agreement—
The one he swore with Abraham our father—
To give us tranquility, release from our enemies' hands,
And freedom to worship him
With devotion and righteousness
All the days of our life.

"And you, little one, will be called the Almighty's prophet.

You'll go in front of the Lord to prepare his paths, to give news of deliverance to his people, and of pardon for their crimes. Because of the tender concern of our God, Heaven's sunrise will dawn upon us, to illuminate those groping in death's shadows and darkness, and to train our feet for the path to peace."

80. The little fellow grew up and matured in spirit. And he stayed on the farm until he began his public ministry in the South.

2.

1. It happened in those days that a proclamation went out from President Augustus that every citizen must register. This was the first registration while Quirinius was Secretary of War. So everybody went to register, each going to his own home town. Joseph too went up from south Georgia from the city of Valdosta, to his home in north Georgia, a place named Gainesville, to register with his bride Mary, who by now was heavily pregnant.

6. While they were there, her time came, and she gave birth to her first boy. She wrapped him in a blanket and laid him in an apple box. (There was no room for them at the hospital.)

8. Now there were some farmers in that section who were up late at night tending their baby chicks. And a messenger from the Lord appeared to them, and evidence of the Lord was shining all about them. It nearly scared the life out of them. And the messenger said to them, "Don't be afraid; for listen, I'm bringing you good news of a great joy in which *all* people will share. Today *your deliverer* was born in the city of David's family. He is the Leader. He is the Lord. And here's a clue for you: you will find the baby wrapped in a blanket and lying in an apple box."

And all of a sudden there was with the messenger a crowd of angels singing God's praises and saying,

"Glory in the highest to God,
And on Earth, *peace* to mankind,
The object of his favor."

15. When the messengers went away from them into the sky, the farmers said to one another, "Let's go to Gainesville and see how all this the Lord has showed us has turned out."

16. So they went just as fast as they could, and found Mary and Joseph, and *the baby lying in an apple box.* Seeing this, they related the story of what had been told them about this little fellow. The people were simply amazed as they listened to what the farmers told them. And Mary clung to all these words, turning them over and over in her memories. The farmers went back home, giving God the credit and singing his praises for all they had seen and heard, exactly as it had been described to them.

21. And when the day came for him to be christened, they named him Jesus, as he was called by the angel before he was conceived.

22. After they had finished carrying out the rules and regulations of the church in regard to the child, they brought him to the bishop in Atlanta to dedicate him to the Lord, just as the scripture said: "Every first baby, if it's a boy, shall be dedicated to the Lord." Also, they wanted to make a thank-offering—as the scripture said—of the equivalent of "a couple of ducks or two fryers."

25. Now then, there was a man in Atlanta whose name was Simon. He was a sincere and devout man, and deeply concerned for the welfare of the world. Being a spirit-led man, he had been assured by the Holy Spirit that he would not die before seeing the Lord's Leader. Guided by the spirit, he came to the First Church. And when the parents brought in the child Jesus for the ceremonies, Simon picked him up in his arms and praised God. He said,

19

"Now let your servant, Almighty Master,
Slip quietly away in peace, as you've said.
For these eyes of mine have seen your deliverance
Which you have made possible for *all* of the people.
It's a light to illuminate the problem of races,
A light to bring honor to your faithful disciples."

33. And his father and mother were really amazed at these things that were said about him. Simon congratulated them and said to Mary his mother, "Listen, this little one is put here for the downfall and uplift of many in the nation, and for a symbol of controversy—your heart, too, will be stabbed with a sword—so that the inner feelings of many hearts may be laid bare."

36. Now Hannah, a lady minister, was there. She was from one of the best families in the South. She was quite old, having lived with her husband for seven years after getting married, and as a widow from then until her present age of eighty-four. She never left the church, worshipping there night and day with prayers and vigils. She came up to them at the same time and gave God's approval, and started talking about the child to all those who were hoping for the nation's deliverance.

39. And when they got through with all the church requirements, they went back to south Georgia, to their own city of Valdosta. And the little fellow grew and became strong. He was plenty smart, and God liked him.

41. Now each year his parents went to Atlanta for the State Conference. So when he was twelve, they went up for the Conference just as they were accustomed to. When it was over, they left for home, but the lad Jesus stayed on in Atlanta without his parents realizing it. Supposing him to be in another car, they went several hours before inquiring about him among friends and relatives. Unable to find him, they returned to Atlanta and continued their search. After a very long time they finally found him at the First Church sitting in the middle of a group of preachers, listening to them and asking them questions. All his hearers were absolutely astounded at his insight and answers. When Joseph and Mary saw this, they were flabbergasted, and his mother said to him, "Listen here, son, why did you treat us like this? Your dad and I have been worried to death looking for you."

49. He said to them, "Why were you looking for me? Didn't you realize that I needed to be with my Father's people?"

50. But they didn't catch on to what he had said to them.

51. He left with them and went back to Valdosta and accepted their guidance. His mother stored up every word in her memory. And Jesus forged ahead both mentally and physically. God liked him, and people did too.

3.

1. Now during the fifteenth year of Tiberius as President, while Pontius Pilate was governor of Georgia, and Herod was governor of Alabama, his brother Philip being governor of Mississippi, and Lysanias still holding out over Arkansas; while Annas and Caiaphas were co-presidents of the Southern Baptist Convention, the word of God came to Zack's boy, John, down on the farm. And he went all around in the rural areas preaching a dipping in water—a symbol of a changed way of life as the basis for getting things straightened out. This was based on a passage from the book of Isaiah the prophet:

"A voice shouts: Make a road for the Lord in the depressed areas, and make it straight.
Every low place shall be filled in,

21

And every hill and high place shall be pushed down.
And the curves shall be straightened out
And the washboard road scraped smooth.
Then *every* human being will share in the good things of God."

7. Here's what he was saying to the crowds who were coming out to get dipped by him: "You sons of snakes, who put the heat on you to run from the fury about to break over your heads? You must give some *proof* that you've had *a change of heart*. And don't start patting one another on the back with that 'we-good-white-people' stuff, because I'm telling you that if God wants to, he can make white-folks out of this pile of rocks. Already the axe is lying at the taproot of the trees, and every tree that doesn't perform some worthwhile function is chopped down and burned up."

10. And the crowds were asking him, "Then what shall we *do* about these problems?"

He answered, "Let him who has two suits *share* with him who has none; and let him who has food do the same thing."

Then the politicians came out to join up, and they asked, "Honorable Teacher, what shall *we* do?"

He said to them, "Cut out your grafts and bribes."

The service men too were asking, "Now how about us? What shall *we* do?"

He told them, "Don't ever use violence on anyone, and don't take advantage of native people—be satisfied with only your government check."

15. Now the people were very excited, and were really searching their hearts about all that John was saying. Some were wondering if perhaps he were the long-awaited Leader. John put a stop to this, saying, "It's true I'm dipping you in water; but somebody is coming who is much stronger than I, whose shoes I'm not worthy to shine. *He* shall dip you in Holy Spirit and fire! He's getting ready to thresh the wheat, and he'll store the grain in the barn and burn up the chaff." With a lot of other sermons like this he was pushing his evangelistic crusade.

19. But when John jumped on Governor Herod for marrying his brother's wife Herodias, and for all the other wicked things he was doing, the governor added even one more item to his list—he locked John up in the jail-house.

21. So it happened that while the people were getting baptized, Jesus too was baptized. And as he prayed, the sky was split and the Holy Spirit in the shape of a dove came down on him. And from the sky came a voice, saying, "You are my dear Son; I'm proud of you."

Now when Jesus started his ministry, he was about thirty years old.[1]

4.

1. So, on fire for God, Jesus returned from his baptism. Then in this spirit he was moved to go into the back woods for forty days, where the Confuser took some cracks at him. During that time he didn't eat anything, so he was hungry when the time was up. Then the Confuser said to him, "So you're God's man, huh? Well, then, tell this rock to become a pone of bread."

Jesus answered back, "A man can't live on bread alone."

5. Then the Confuser took him up and showed him, in the twinkling of an eye, all the countries of the civilized world. And he said, "Look here, all this power and glory has been turned over to me, and to anybody I want to share it with. Now if you'll just let *me* be boss, I'll put you in charge and turn everything over to you."

---

[1]In the Greek text, Jesus' family tree is inserted here, but we have omitted it as unnecessary for the purposes of this translation.

Jesus shot back, "The scripture says, 'You shall let the Lord your God be your boss, and you shall give your loyalty to him alone."

9. The Confuser then brought him into Atlanta, and put him on the steeple of the First Church, and said, "Okay, you're God's man. Now jump down from here, because you know the scripture says, 'He will give orders to his angels to keep close watch on you,' and also, 'They'll carry you along on their hands to keep you from stumping your toe on a rock.' "

Jesus told him straight, "It also says, 'Don't make a fool out of the Lord your God.' "

13. So when the Confuser got through giving him the works, he left him for a while. Then Jesus, spiritually invigorated, returned to south Georgia, and the news of him spread through the whole area. He was speaking in their churches, and the people respected him. But he went to Valdosta, where he had grown up, and as he was in the habit of doing, he went to church on Sunday. They invited him to preach, so he got up to read the scripture and found the place in the book of Isaiah where it says:

"The Lord's spirit is on me;
He has ordained me to break the good news to the poor people.
He has sent me to proclaim freedom for the oppressed,
And sight for the blind,
To help those who have been grievously insulted to find dignity;
To proclaim the Lord's new era."

20. Then he closed the Bible, and handed it to the assistant minister. The eyes of everybody in the congregation were glued on him. He began by saying,

"This very day this Scripture has become a reality in your presence."

They all said, "Amen," and were amazed at the eloquent words

24

flowing from his mouth. They whispered to one another, "Can this really be old Joe's boy?"

23. Then he continued, "Surely some of you will cite to me the old proverb, 'Doctor, take your own medicine. Let us see you do right here in your home town all the things we heard you did in Columbus.' Well, to tell the truth, no prophet is welcome in his own home town. And I'm telling you straight, there were a lot of *white* widows in Georgia during the time of Elijah, when the skies were locked up for three years and six months, and there was a great drought everywhere, but Elijah didn't stay with any of *them.* Instead, he stayed with a *Negro* woman over in Terrell County. And there were a lot of sick *white* people during the time of the great preacher Elisha, but he didn't heal any of *them*—only Naaman the African."

28. When they heard that, the whole congregation blew a gasket. They jumped up, ran him out of town, and dragged him to the top of the hill on which their city was built, with the intention of pushing him off. But he got up and walked right through the middle of the whole mob and went on his way.

31. And he came to Macon, the county seat of Bibb County. And he was speaking there every Sunday. They were quite amazed at his teachings, because there was a note of authority in his words. One day at church there was a man who had the spirit of a filthy devil, and he bellowed out as loud as he could, "Hey, Jesus, you Valdostan squirt, what you got agin us? Have you come up here to stir up trouble for us? I know who you are, you Holy Joe."

35. Then Jesus rebuked him and said, "Shut up and come out of that man." And the filthy spirit convulsed him right in front of everybody, but came out of him without leaving a scratch.

A wonderment came over all, and they whispered back and forth, "Well, what do you know about that? He orders the filthy devils around as though he has a right to, and they come out!" And news dispatches about him went out to all parts of the country.

38. So he left the church and went home with Simon. Now Simon's mother-in-law was sick with a high fever, so they spoke to him about her. He leaned over her and rebuked the fever, and it left her. She got up right away and started waiting on them.

40. As the sun set, all those who had loved ones who were sick with various diseases brought them to him. He put his hands on each one of them and made them well. Even devils were coming out of a lot of them, calling and crying out, "So you're God's man, huh?" He got after them and wouldn't even let them say a word, because they really knew that he was God's man.

42. When day came, he left and went to a remote place. But the crowds were looking for him and came to where he was. They held on to him to keep him from leaving them. But he said, "I've got to spread the good news of the God Movement to a lot of other cities. This is what I've been sent to do." And he was preaching in the churches of Georgia.

5.

1. While he was standing beside Lake Lanier, a crowd gathered around him to hear the word of God. He saw two little boats beside the lake, whose owners had left them while they washed their nets. He got into one of the boats, which belonged to Simon, and asked him to shove off a little way from the bank. Then he sat down in the boat and taught the crowds. When he had finished, he said to Simon, "Go out where it's deep, and let down your nets for a haul."

Simon answered, "Mister, we've worked our heads off all night long and haven't caught a thing; but, if you say so, I'll put out the nets."

They did, and caught such a slew of fish that their nets started busting. So they yelled to their buddies in the other boat to come quick and lend them a hand. They came, and they filled both little boats so full they almost sank.

When Simon (Rock) saw it all, he got down on his knees before Jesus and said, "Don't waste your time on a bum like me, sir!" For he and his buddies were bug-eyed because of the big wad of fish they had caught. Simon's business partners, Jim and Jack Zebedee, were also amazed.

Then Jesus said to Simon, "Don't worry about it. From now on you'll fish for *men*." And when they got their boats back to shore, they gave up everything and started living like him.

12. Now it happened that while he was in one of the cities, a man with bad sores saw Jesus and begged him, saying, "Sir, if *you want* to, you are able to heal me." Jesus reached out and touched him and said, "I do want to BE HEALED." And right away the sores left him. Then he told the man not to go spreading the word around, but to tell only the preacher, and to make a thank-offering for his healing, as the Bible said. This would be convincing evidence for the ministers. But instead, word of him was spread all over everywhere, and big crowds came together to hear, and to be healed of their illnesses. But he would leave and go to the country to pray.

17. It so happened on one of the days when he was teaching that there was a convention of church members and Sunday School teachers from the little towns all over Alabama and Georgia and from around Atlanta. And he felt the power of God moving in him to heal. Soon some men came carrying a paralyzed man on a stretcher, and they tried to get in to where Jesus was so they could put the man in front of him. When they couldn't get in because of the big crowd, they went up on the roof, took up some

27

tiles and let the stretcher down just in front of Jesus. Seeing the way they had put their faith into action, he said, "Fellow, your sins are forgiven."

21. Then the church officials and convention delegates began raising cain about it, saying, "Who is this guy that's saying such unorthodox things? Who but God alone has the right to forgive sins?"

Jesus overheard their arguments and asked them, "Why do you allow such arguments to enter your mind? Which is easier, to say, 'Your sins are forgiven' or to say 'Get up and walk'? But to make it clear to you that the son of man has the right on earth to forgive sins"—he said to the paralyzed man—"Get up, pick up your stretcher and run along home."

Right away he got up in front of everybody, picked up the stretcher he had been lying on, and went home shouting God's praises. The crowd went into ecstasy and started shouting God's praises too. They were filled with awe, and said, "We've seen something today so wonderful we can't understand it."

27. He left after that, and he saw a Yankee by the name of Levi, working for the Internal Revenue Service. And Jesus said to him, "Walk in this way with me." He got up, quit his job with the government, and started walking in the way with him.

29. And Levi gave a big reception for him at his house. Now there were quite a few Yankees and others sitting around with them. And the church members and officials said to Jesus' students, "How come you all eating and socializing with Yankees and niggers?"

Jesus picked it up and told them, "Healthy people don't need a doctor—only the sick do. I haven't come to challenge the 'saved' people to a new way of walking—only the 'sinners.' "

33. Then they said to him, "John's followers go to church every Sunday and say their prayers, just like all good church members do. But your crowd, they're acting like they *enjoy* their religion!"

Jesus said to them, "Do the best men at a wedding look gloomy while they're standing beside the groom at the ceremony? But, the time will come when the groom will be parted from them. *Then* they will be sad on that occasion."[2]

36. He also gave them this comparison: "No housewife ever uses new, unshrunk material to patch an old dress. If she does, the new will shrink and pull, and won't match the old material. And nobody ever puts new, fermenting wine in old, brittle, plastic bottles. If he does, the new wine will pop the old bottles, and the wine will be wasted and the bottles ruined. But new wine is put into new, strong bottles. And nobody who is accustomed to drinking old wine wants to try out the new, because he says, 'The old is good enough for me.'"

6.

1. One Sunday as he was going through a grain field, his students were picking some heads, rubbing out the grain with their hands and eating it. Some church members said, "How come you all doing what's wrong to do on a Sunday?"

Jesus replied, "Haven't you ever read in the Bible what David did when he and those with him were hungry? How he went into the church house and got the communion bread, which legally belongs to the preachers, and ate it and shared it with those with him?"

So he said to them, "The son of man has authority over 'Sunday.'"

On another Sunday he went into a church to preach. And a man was there whose right hand was dried up. The deacons and members were keeping an eye on Jesus to see if he would heal on a Sunday, so they might have a charge to bring against him. Since

---

[2]It is possible that this is not a reference to his crucifixion, but an indictment of their own "groomless" and therefore joyless condition.

29

he himself already knew their plottings, he said to the man with the dried-up hand, "Come and stand up here in front of everybody." So he came and stood. Then Jesus said to them, "Let me ask you all, is it all right to do good or to do bad on Sunday? To save a life or to destroy it?"

He cut his eyes around on all of them, and said to the man, "STRETCH OUT YOUR HAND." He did so, and his hand was perfectly normal. But they pitched a fit and started conferring with each other as to what in the world they would do to Jesus.

12. During those days he went out into a mountain to pray, and all night long he continued in prayer to God. At dawn he called up his students, and from them he selected twelve, whom he designated "ambassadors." They were: Simon (whom he also called Rock) and his brother Andy; Jim and Jack, and Phil and Barth, and Matt and Tom, and Jim Alphaeus, and Simon the Rebel, and Judas Jameson, and Judas Iscariot—who turned him in.

17. And he came down with them and stood at the foot of the hill, along with quite a number of his students and a big crowd of people from all over Georgia and around Atlanta, and even as far away as Virginia. They came to listen to him and to be healed from their illnesses. And those who were literally swarming with filthy spirits were cured. The whole crowd was trying to touch him, because power flowed out of him and he healed them one and all.

20. Then he fastened his eyes on his students and said to them: "The poor are God's people, because the God Movement is yours.

"You who are now hungering are God's people, because you will be filled.

"You who are now weeping are God's people, because you will laugh.

"You are God's people when others hate you and shun you and pick on you and blacklist you just because you bear the name of

30

the son of man. Be happy at that time and jump for joy, for your spiritual pay is high. Why, their fathers did the very same things to the men of God of their day.

BUT—

"It will be hell[3] for you rich people, because you've had your fling.

"It will be hell for you whose bellies are full now, because you'll go hungry.

"It will be hell for you who are so gay now, because you will sob and weep.

"It will be hell for you when everybody speaks highly of you, for their fathers said the very same things about the phony preachers.

27. "But let me tell you people something: Love your enemies, deal kindly with those who hate you, give your blessings to those who give you their cursing, pray for those insulting you. When somebody slaps you on one side of the face, offer the other side too. And if a guy takes your shirt, don't stop him from taking your undershirt. Give to every beggar, and don't ask someone who takes your stuff to bring it back. Just as you want people to act towards you, you act the same way towards them. If you love those who love you, what's your advantage? Even non-Christians love those who love them. If you are kind to those who are kind to you, what's your advantage? Even non-Christians do that. And if you lend with the hope of getting it all back, what's your advantage? Even non-Christians lend to those who'll pay it all back. But *you all*, love your enemies, and be kind, and lend, expecting nothing. And you'll get plenty of 'pay'; you'll be the spittin' image of the Almighty, who himself is friendly towards the unlovely and the mean. Be tender, just as your Father is tender. Don't blame, and you won't be blamed. Don't run others down, and they won't run

---

[3]The Greek word, generally translated as "woe," is the sound of an agonizing groan, "o-o-oh," as from someone in great anguish or torment, as "in hell."

you down. Free others, and you shall be freed; give, and it shall be given to you in full measure, tromped down, shaken down, running over into your heart. For it will be measured out to you in your own measuring basket."

39. So he gave them this Comparison: "A blind man can't guide a blind man, can he? Won't they both fall in a hole? Nor is a student over the teacher. He alone who has completed school qualifies as a teacher.

41. "Now why do you keep looking at the splinter in your brother's eye, and pay no attention to the plank in your own eye? How do you have the nerve to say to your brother, 'Brother, please let me pick the splinter out of your eye,' without even noticing the *plank* in your eye? You phony, first get the plank from your eye, and then you'll see better to pick the splinter from your brother's eye.

43. "For a cultivated tree doesn't bear wild fruit, nor does a wild tree bear cultivated fruit. So, each tree may be known by the kind of fruit it produces. Also, people don't pick peaches from briars or grapes from a haw bush. A good man, from the good things stored in his heart, produces the good deed, while the mean person, from the mean things stored in his heart, produces the mean act. For the tongue is powered by the overflow from the heart.

46. "Now why are you calling me 'Your honor, this,' and 'Your honor, that,' and don't carry out my orders? Anyone who comes before me and hears my orders and carries them out, I'll tell you who he is like. He is like a man building a house, who dug down and went deep, and laid the foundation on bedrock. At flood-time the river went ripping at that house, and it couldn't even budge it, because it was solidly built. But he who has heard my orders and hasn't done anything about them, is like a man who built a house on the ground without a foundation. The river ripped at it, and right away it caved in, and there was great damage to that house."

7.

1. When he finished pounding his points into the ears of the crowd, he went to Columbus. Now the servant of a Jewish army captain was so sick he was about to die. The captain loved him very much, so when he heard about Jesus he sent some of the leading citizens of the city to ask Jesus to come and save his servant's life. Upon their arrival they strongly urged Jesus to come, saying, "The man asking you to do this is a mighty fine fellow. He loves our denomination, and made a very substantial gift to our church-building program." So Jesus went with them.

6. While he was still quite a distance from the house, the army captain sent some other friends to say to Jesus, "Sir, don't put yourself out, because I'm not worthy that you should come to my house. I didn't think I was good enough even to come to you personally. So just give the order, and my dear one will be healed. For I, too, am a man with authority, having soldiers under my command, and I say to one, 'Go there' and he goes, and to another, 'Come here,' and he comes, and to my servant, 'Do this,' and he does it."

9. When Jesus heard this he was simply amazed, and turning to the crowd following him he said, "Never have I found such faith, even among the good 'saved' church people." And when the ones who had been sent got back to the house they found the servant fully recovered.

11. Soon after that he went to the city of Thomaston, and he was accompanied by his students and a large group of others. As he neared the outskirts of the city, he saw the funeral procession for a man who was his mother's only son—and she was a widow.

Quite a number of people from the city were in the procession. When the Master saw her, he was deeply moved, and he said to her, "Please don't cry any more." Then he went over and touched the casket. The pallbearers stopped, and he said, "Young fellow, I'm telling you to GET UP." And the corpse sat up and started talking! Then Jesus returned him to his mother.

16. And wonder came over everybody, and they praised God, saying, "A truly great man of God has been raised up among us," and "God has paid a visit to his people." And this news of him went out through Georgia and the surrounding states.

18. Now John's students reported to him all that was happening, and so he called two of them and sent them to the Master with this message: "Are *you* the Expected One, or are we to wait for someone else?" When the men approached Jesus they said, "John the Baptizer sent us to you to inquire if *you* are the Expected One, or if we should wait for another?"

At that time he was healing many people of their illnesses and plagues and mean spirits, and he was joyfully giving sight to lots of blind people.

So he said to them, "Please go back and tell John what you've just seen and heard—tell him the blind are seeing, the crippled are walking, the lepers are getting well, the deaf are hearing, the dead are rising, and the poor are getting the good word. Tell him, too, that he is a great and good man who is not offended by my approach to things."

24. After John's messengers left, he began talking to the group about John. "What did you expect to see when you went out to the backwoods? A bamboo blown this way and that by the wind? Really, what *did* you expect to see when you went out? A man dressed up in his Sunday best? Listen, people who wear expensive clothes and eat fine food are among the well-to-do. Really, now, what did you expect when you went out? A man of God? Of course! And brother, I'm telling you, *what* a man of God! He's the one to whom this scripture refers:

'I'm sending my agent to precede you;
He'll get everything ready for your coming.'

I tell you right now, there has never been a mother's son greater than John. *But, the tiniest baby in the God Movement is greater than he!"*

29. Now when the whole group, including some Yankees who had been initiated into John's movement, heard what Jesus said, they agreed that this was right, before God. But the church members and the theologians, who had not joined his Movement, refused to accept *this* approach as God's will for themselves.

31. "So then, with what shall I compare the people of this day, and what are they like? I know, they are like *children* playing in the streets, and shouting at each other, 'We put on some jazz, but you wouldn't dance; so we put on funeral music, but you wouldn't go into mourning.' For John the Baptizer offered you a harsh, rugged life, and you say, 'The guy is nuts.' I, the son of man, offer you laughter and joy, and you say, 'Look at that man, a gadfly and a jitter-bug, a friend of Yankees and a nigger-lover.' So, if *intelligence* can be judged by all that it produces, well—!"

36. A certain church member invited him home for dinner. He accepted and went into the church member's house and sat down. Then a shady lady of the town, who had heard that Jesus was being entertained at the church member's home, bought a bottle of high-priced perfume. She sat at his feet sobbing, and her tears began to wet his feet. She dried them with her long hair and kissed his feet and dabbed on some of the perfume.

When the church member who had invited him saw what was going on, he thought to himself, "If this fellow were a real man of God, he would recognize the kind of woman that's fondling him and know that she's a shady character."

Then Jesus said to him, "Simon, I want to talk with you about something."

He said, "Why sure, Doctor, go right ahead."

"Two men were in debt to a certain banker. One owed five hundred dollars, the other fifty. When neither of them could pay up, the banker wrote off the debt of both. Which of the two would you think was the more grateful?"

Simon scratched his head and said, "Why, I suppose it was the one who was relieved of the larger debt."

Jesus said to him, "Right you are!" Then he turned to the lady and said to Simon, "Do you see this lady? When I came into your home, *you* didn't even give me *water* for my feet, but *she* has bathed my feet with her *tears* and dried them with her hair. You didn't even shake *hands* with me, but she, ever since she got here, has lovingly kissed my *feet*. So let me point out to you, Simon, that she has been relieved of a heavy load of sin, as evidenced by her great gratitude."

Then he said to her, "Your sins are gone."

And the guests at the table whispered among themselves, "Who does he think he is—forgiving sins!"

He said to the lady, "What you've just done has been the making of you; keep it up—with my blessing."

8.

1. Following this, he made a trip from city to city, speaking and explaining the ideas of the God Movement. The Twelve went with him, and so did some women who had been cured of their spirits of weakness and meanness—Mary, whom everyone called "that Magdala girl," and who had been given up for lost, and Jo Ann, the wife of Kuza, Governor Herod's assistant, and Susan and quite a few others—all of whom were sharing what they had, in order to provide for the whole group.

4. Now when a crowd of people from all over had gathered around him, he gave them a Comparison: "A farmer went out to plant his seed. As he planted, some seed fell on the path where they were walked on, and the birds came and ate them. Some seed fell on the rock, and though they sprouted, they dried up from lack of moisture. Still others landed in the middle of a briar patch, and the briars that came up with them choked them out. And others fell on the rich dirt and grew and yielded a hundred times over." He finished by saying, "Give this *careful* consideration."

9. Then his students asked him what was the meaning of the Comparison. He said, "You all have been let in on the secrets of the God Movement, but it is necessary to explain it to others with Comparisons, so that while they're looking they won't catch on, and while they're listening, they won't suspect anything.

"But here's the meaning of the Comparison. The seed are God's ideas. The 'path' seed represent ideas that are heard by people who let the Confuser come and snatch the ideas from their hearts, without their ever acting on them and being helped. The 'rock' seed are the ideas which, when heard, are gladly received—but by people who have no deep roots. They live by them for a while, and when the time of real testing comes, they chicken out. The 'briar patch' seed are the ideas which are heard by busy people and are choked out by the distractions and money-making and pleasure-seeking of life, so the ideas just never mature. The 'rich dirt' seed are the ones which lie in the hearts of brave and good people who, when they hear the ideas, hold on to them and patiently spread them.

16. "Nobody ever turns on a light and covers it with a pot, or slides it under a bed. Instead, they put it on a table so that people entering the room will be able to see. So, there's no one in the background now who will not be brought to the front, and no one who is insignificant who won't be recognized and brought up front. Be careful, then, how you respond. For whoever gets on the ball will be encouraged all the more, and whoever sits on his hands will have even what little he seems to have, taken away from him."

19. Now his mother and brothers came to him but were unable to reach him because of the crowd. So somebody told him, "Your mother and brothers are outside trying to get in touch with you." His reply was, "My mother and my brothers are they who hear God's ideas and act on them."

22. It so happened on one of those days that he and his students got in a boat, and he said to them, "Let's go over to the other side of the lake." They set out, and while they were sailing, he went to sleep. A great windstorm arose on the lake, and they began shipping water and sinking. They rushed to him and roused him and said, "Captain, Captain, we're going down!" He got up quickly and told the wind and towering waves to hush. They quieted down, and it became calm. He then said to his students, "What happened to your faith?" They were scared to death and in amazement said to each other, "What a man! He orders the wind and water around, and they obey him!"

26. They sailed on over to Gerasa County, Alabama, which is across the lake from Georgia. When he got out on land, he was met by a city man who had a "demon." For a long time he had worn no clothing and wouldn't stay in a house but in a cemetery. When he saw Jesus, he stood in front of him and yelled and shouted at the top of his lungs, "What you got against me, Jesus, you God's holy boy? I warn you, don't you put the screws on me." (For Jesus was telling the mean spirit to come out of the man, because it frequently convulsed him, and he had to be placed under guard, shackled and handcuffed. But he broke loose and was driven by the "demon" into the back woods.)

So Jesus asked him, "What's your name?"

He said, "Multitude," since a whole slew of demons had entered him.

Then they started begging him not to order them into exile.
Now, there on the hillside a large herd of hogs was being fed, so
the demons begged him to let them go into them. He permitted
them, and the demons rushed out of the man and into the hogs.
When they did, the whole herd went tearing down the slope and
into the lake and were drowned. When the herdsmen saw what
had happened, they ran like mad and told it to both farmers and
city people. Everybody flocked out to gawk, and they came to Jesus
and found the man from whom the demons had departed, sitting
at Jesus' feet, fully clothed and completely sane. It just scared the
daylights out of them, especially when the herdsmen kept telling
them how the demon-man had been cured. So all the people in
that part of Alabama asked him to go away and let them alone,
because they were so scared they were shaking all over.

38. When he got into the boat to leave, the man from whom the
demons had departed asked to go with him. But he turned him
down and said, "Go back home and tell them about all that God
has done for you." So he went through the whole city, speaking on
what Jesus did for him.

40. After Jesus got back, a crowd was waiting for him, for
they had been anxiously looking for him. And there came a man
by the name of Jarrell, who was pastor of the local church. He
greeted Jesus, and then urged him to come home with him, because
his twelve-year-old daughter—his only child—was at the point of
death. As Jesus went, the crowd packed tight around him. And a
lady, who had been bleeding for twelve years and hadn't been able
to find anyone who could heal her, came up behind him and
touched his pants leg. And right away her bleeding stopped.

Jesus said, "Who touched me?"

When they all denied it, Rock said, "Chief, the whole crowd is
pushing and shoving you."

But Jesus said, "Somebody touched me, because I felt power
flowing out of me."

When the lady saw that the cat was out of the bag, she came quivering and bowing low before him. She told him in front of the whole crowd why she had touched him, and how she had been cured on the spot. He said to her, "My dear daughter, your trustful action has been the saving of you. Keep it up—with my blessing."

49. Even as he was talking, somebody came from the minister's house and said, "Your daughter has died. There's no need to trouble the teacher any further."

When Jesus heard that, he said to Jarrell, "Don't worry; just have faith and she will be all right."

51. Arriving at the house, he allowed no one to go in except Rock and Jack and Jim, and the father and mother of the child. Everybody was crying and carrying on, so he said, "You all quit crying; she isn't dead, she's just asleep."

They took it as a crude joke, because they *knew* she was dead. He then took her by the hand and called out to her, "Young lady, GET UP!" And she began breathing and immediately she stood up. He then told them to give her something to eat. Her parents were astounded, but he urged them not to tell anyone what had happened.

9.

1. Summoning the Twelve, he gave them power and authority over all demon cases and to cure diseases. And he sent them out to speak on the God Movement and to heal. He said to them, "Take nothing on your trip—no sleeping bag, no suitcase, no bread, no money, not even two suits. When you are invited to a home, you may use it as a base of operations. If no one will invite you, leave that city without so much as a particle of dust from it clinging to your feet, as evidence to them that you've taken nothing of theirs."

6. So they left, and went through all the towns, spreading the good news and healing everywhere. Word reached Governor

Herod about all that was happening, and he was flabbergasted. For it was reported by some that John was raised from the dead, by others that Elijah had reappeared, and by still others that one of the old-time men of God had come back. Herod said, "John's head I chopped off, but who is this fellow I'm hearing so much about?" And he was anxious to get a good look at him.

10. Soon the disciples returned and described to him all that they had done. He took them and left privately for a city named Griffin. The crowds found out about it, and followed him along the way. So he let them come to him and he was explaining to them the God Movement, and curing those who were sick. As the end of the day drew near, the Twelve said to him, "Dismiss the crowd, so they can go to the neighboring cafes and motels to find food and lodging, because there's nothing around out here."

He said to them, "*You* all go ahead and feed them."

But they said, "Between all of us there's no more than five boxes of crackers and two cans of sardines. Or do you mean that we should go and *buy* supplies for all *this* crowd?" (For there were about five thousand people.)

"Tell them to sit down in groups of about fifty," he said to his students.

They did this, and everybody sat down. He then asked for the five boxes of crackers and the two cans of sardines, and when he had given thanks, he opened them and gave them to the students to distribute to the crowd. All ate and had plenty, and there were twelve trays full, left uneaten.

18. It so happened that while he was praying alone, his students gathered around him. He put this question to them: "Who do the people think I am?"

They replied, "Some think you're John the Baptizer, others think you're Elijah, while still others believe that one of the old-time men of God has arisen."

He then asked, "How about you all—who do *you* say I am?"

Rock spoke up. "God's appointed Leader," he said.

At this he told them that they absolutely must not spread this word around, "because," he said, "it is now a certainty that the son of man will suffer greatly and be scorned by the church officials and ministers and scholars, and be killed, and on the third day be raised."

23. Then he said, so everybody could hear, "If anybody really wants to share my way of life, let him have no regard for his own welfare, and let him risk his life every day and walk the way with me. Whoever puts his own life first shall lose it. But whoever lays his life on the line for me shall come out on top. For what has a man gained if he gets the whole world, and his own life is broken or destroyed in the process? If anyone is embarrassed around me and my ideas, the son of man will be embarrassed to have him around at his 'coronation' by the Father, and the dedicated attendants. For I'm telling you a fact: there are some standing right here who won't die before they see the God Movement."

28. About eight days after speaking these words, he took Rock and Jack and Jim and went into the mountains to pray. It so happened that while he was praying, the whole appearance of his face became different, and his clothes were so white they hurt your eyes. And lo and behold, two men were carrying on a conversation with him! They were Moses and Elijah in their heavenly form and they were talking with him about *his* EXODUS—which he was soon to get into full swing in Atlanta.

32. Now Rock and those with him were awfully sleepy, but this got them so wide awake that they saw his wondrous appearance, as well as that of the men standing beside him. And as the two were leaving Jesus, Rock said to him, "Skipper, it's wonderful for us to be here, perfectly wonderful. So let's build three chapels, one for you, one for Moses, and one for Elijah"—without even realizing what he was saying.

34. He had hardly finished talking when a cloud came up and enveloped them. They were dreadfully frightened as they entered the cloud, and then out of the cloud came a voice, saying, *"This is my dear Son; do what he tells you."* After the voice, no one was there but Jesus. They all kept quiet, and during those days they didn't tell a soul what they had seen.

37. The next day they came down from the mountain and a large crowd met him. One of the men in the crowd called out for help, saying, "Doctor, please take a look at my son, my only child. He has a seizure, and all of a sudden he screams, and he writhes and foams at the mouth. He gets over it with great difficulty, and it just crushes him. I asked your students to do something, but they couldn't."

Jesus cried out, "You distrustful and misguided people, how much longer shall I put up with you? Bring your boy here."

Even as he was coming, the boy had another seizure and went into convulsions. Jesus quieted the abnormal spirit, and healed the lad and gave him back to his father. And all were astonished at the magnificence of God.

43. Now while they were marvelling at all the things he was doing, he said to his students, "You all let these words sink into your ears: *the son of man is about to be turned over to the authorities."* But they didn't grasp this saying at all. Its meaning was so hidden from them that they didn't catch on, and they were afraid to ask him to explain what he had said.

46. Then they got into a heated discussion as to which one of them was the most important. So Jesus—realizing what the motives behind the argument were—took a child and stood him in front of them and said, "Anyone in my fellowship who accepts this youngster accepts me, and anyone who accepts me, accepts him who commissioned me. Among *you,* the littlest one is important."

49. Jack spoke up and said, "Skipper, we saw somebody using your name to cast out demons, and we put a stop to it, because he didn't belong to our group."

But Jesus told him, "Don't stop him, for if someone isn't opposed to you, he is for you."

51. Now when the days for his arrest approached, he set his heart on going to Atlanta. He sent the arrangements committee on ahead, and on the way they stopped in a black community to find accommodations. But they refused to accept Jesus' party, because there were white people in it.[4]

When Jim and Jack saw this, they said, "Sir, do you want us to give them the 'fire-from-heaven' treatment and bump 'em off?" But Jesus turned and scolded them, and they went on to another town.

57. While they were going along the way, somebody said to him, "I'll live your life, regardless of where it takes me."

Jesus replied, "Foxes have dens, and the birds of the sky have nests, but the son of man has nowhere to hang his hat."

Then he said to another, "Share my life."

"Okay," he said, "but let me first discharge my family obligations."[5]

Jesus told him, "Let the people of the world care for themselves, but *you*, you spend your time promoting the God Movement."

Still another said, "I will share your life, sir, but let me first work things out with my relatives."[6]

To him Jesus replied, "No man who commits himself to a course of action, and then keeps looking for a way out of it, is fit material for the God Movement."

---

[4]Literally, the phrase is, "Because he (his party) was headed towards Jerusalem." Since the Jews refused to serve Samaritans in Jerusalem, the Samaritans reciprocated by refusing service to Jews who stopped in Samaria.

[5]Literally, "Let me first bury my father." This is not a request to attend his father's funeral. To "bury one's father" meant to take care of the father until he died, which might require many years. His request then is to fulfill his duties to his father.

[6]Obviously, this fellow wants to draw up a legal contract protecting his family rights in the event the venture with Jesus didn't pan out.

10.

1. After this, the Lord picked out seventy others and sent them in pairs to precede him into every city and place where he himself was about to go. Briefing them, he said, "There is a big harvest but few workers. Make your request to the harvest-master that he provide workers for his harvest. Now let's get on the move. Listen, I'm sending you out like sheep surrounded by a pack of wolves. Don't carry a suitcase or a wallet or shoes. And don't stop and gab with everybody you meet. When you go into a home, first greet them by wishing them peace. If a truly peaceful man is there, your peace will take root in him; if there isn't, it will bounce back on you. Stay in the same house, eating and drinking whatever they provide for you, for a worker is entitled to his pay. Don't change around from one home to another. And to whatever city you go— and they accept you—eat what's set before you and heal the sick in the town. And keep telling them, 'The God Movement is confronting you.' But if you go to a city and they *won't* accept you, go out on the main streets and say, 'We are shaking off every particle of dust from your city that's sticking to our feet. But let this be clear to you: *the God Movement is here.*' I'm telling you, when that happens it will be easier on Las Vegas than on that city.

13. "It will be hell for you, Columbus. It will be hell for you, Albany. If Berlin and London had seen as many evidences of God's activity as you have, they would have humbly changed their ways a long time ago. But Berlin and London will have it easier in the Judgment than you. And you, Savannah, do you think you'll be praised to the skies? You'll be sent to hell!

"He who listens to you, listens to me, and who rejects you, rejects me. And who rejects me, rejects Him who sent me."

17. So the seventy went out and later returned with joy, saying, "Sir, even the most devilish ones gave in to us when we approached them in your name."

He said to them, "Yes, and I saw the whole satanic structure smashed like a bolt of lightning from the sky. Look here, I've given you the ability to trample on 'snakes and scorpions,' and on the power-structure of the opposition, and nothing will be able to stop you. But don't get all hepped up just because the devilish guys gave in to you; instead, you should be happy that you're enrolled in a spiritual cause."

21. At that same time the Holy Spirit flooded him with deep joy, and he said, "I fully admit to you, Lord of heaven and earth, that you've kept these things from the egg-heads and the worldly-wise, and have let trustful 'babies' in on them. Indeed, O Father, this is the way it seemed best to you."

Then turning to his students, he said, "My Father has left everything up to me. No one but the Father truly knows the Son, and no one but the Son and whoever else he wishes to let in on it, truly knows the Father." He privately said to his students, "You are indeed fortunate to be seeing what you see. For I'm telling you, many sincere ministers and statesmen would have given almost anything to see what you're looking at but they never saw it, and to hear what you're hearing but they never heard it."

25. One day a teacher of an adult Bible class got up and tested him with this question: "Doctor, what does one do to be saved?"

Jesus replied, "What does the Bible say? How do you interpret it?"

The teacher answered, "Love the Lord your God with all your heart and with all your soul and with all your physical strength and with all your mind; and love your neighbor as yourself."

"That is correct," answered Jesus. "Make a habit of this and you'll be saved."

But the Sunday school teacher, trying to save face, asked, "But ... er ... but ... just who *is* my neighbor?"

Then Jesus laid into him and said, "A man was going from Atlanta to Albany and some gangsters held him up. When they had robbed him of his wallet and brand-new suit, they beat him up and drove off in his car, leaving him unconscious on the shoulder of the highway.

"Now it just so happened that a white preacher was going down that same highway. When he saw the fellow, he stepped on the gas and went scooting by.[7]

"Shortly afterwards a white Gospel song leader came down the road, and when he saw what had happened, he too stepped on the gas.[8]

"Then a black man traveling that way came upon the fellow, and what he saw moved him to tears. He stopped and bound up his wounds as best he could, drew some water from his water-jug to wipe away the blood and then laid him on the back seat.[9] He drove on into Albany and took him to the hospital and said to the nurse, 'You all take good care of this white man I found on the highway. Here's the only two dollars I got, but you all keep account of what he owes, and if he can't pay it, I'll settle up with you when I make a pay-day.'

"Now if you had been the man held up by the gangsters, which of these three—the white preacher, the white song leader, or the black man—would you consider to have been your neighbor?"

The teacher of the adult Bible class said, "Why, of course, the nig—I mean, er... well, er... the one who treated me kindly."

Jesus said, "Well, then, *you* get going and start living like that!"

38. Journeying along, they came to a certain town, and a lady by the name of Martha invited him to her home. She had a sister

[7]His homiletical mind probably made the following outline: 1. I do not know the man. 2. I do not wish to get involved in any court proceedings. 3. I don't want to get blood on my new upholstering. 4. The man's lack of proper clothing would embarrass me upon my arrival in town. 5. And finally, brethren, a minister must never be late for worship services.

[8]What his thoughts were we'll never know, but as he whizzed past, he may have been whistling, "Brighten the corner, where you are."

[9]All the while his thoughts may have been along this line: "Somebody's robbed you; yeah, I know about that, I been robbed, too. And they done beat you up bad; I know, I been beat up, too. And everybody just go right on by and leave you laying here hurting. Yeah, I know. They pass me by, too."

named Mary, who sat down beside Jesus and listened eagerly to his ideas. All the while, Martha was rushing around trying to get everything ready. Unable to stand it any longer, she went in and said, "Sir, doesn't it make any difference to you that my sister has left all the serving up to me? Tell her to come lend me a hand!"

Jesus answered, "Martha! Martha! You're worrying and fretting about a lot of things, when a few or even one is plenty. Now Mary has made a wise choice, which shall not be denied her."

11.

1. It so happened that he was in a certain place praying, and when he had finished, one of his students said to him, "Sir, teach us to pray, just as John taught his students."

He said to them, "When you pray, say, 'Father, may your name be taken seriously. May your Movement spread. Sustaining bread grant us each day. And free us from our sins, even as we release everyone indebted to us. And don't let us get all tangled up.'"

5. He went on to say, "Suppose you have a friend who comes to you in the middle of the night and says, 'Hey neighbor, how about lending me three loaves of bread. A friend of mine has just arrived at my house, and I don't have anything to serve him.' Then you'll call out from inside the house, 'Please don't disturb me! I've already locked the door and have got all the kids to sleep. I can't get up and let you have anything.' I really believe that even though you won't get up and let him have something out of friendship for him, you will crawl out and let him have whatever he needs if he keeps yelling and pounding on the door."

"So that's why I'm telling you, start asking and it will be given to you; start looking, and you will find; start knocking, and it will be opened to you. For every asker receives, every seeker finds, and to every one who knocks the door is opened. Is there any father among you who, when his son shall ask him for a fish, will give him a snake instead? Or if he should ask for an egg, will he give him a scorpion? Well, then, if you—sinful as you are—are capable of making good gifts to your children, how much more will the spiritual Father give the Holy Spirit to all who ask him?"

14. And he was throwing out a mean spirit from a man who couldn't talk. When the mean spirit came out, the man was able to speak. People were simply amazed at this, yet some of them said, "He's prying loose the mean spirits in the name of Dung-King, the leader of all mean spirits." Still others taunted him and tried to get him to work a miracle. But he knew what they were up to, and said to them, "Any kingdom that's split up into opposing sides will go on the rocks, and a household so divided will bust up. All right, you say I'm throwing out mean spirits with the help of Dung-King. Then if Satan is opposing himself, how can his kingdom hold together? And further, if I am *throwing out* mean spirits with Dung-King's help, with whose help are *your* sons throwing them out? Your sons, therefore, will be the evidence that will convict you.[10]

"But now, if I am throwing out devils with the help of *God's* finger, then God's Movement is squarely confronting you."[11]

21. "When a man who relies on force maintains a heavy guard around his place, his property is undisturbed. But if somebody comes against him with a superior force, and conquers him, then he'll carry off all the equipment the man thought would defend him, and parcel out the loot.

"If you're not with me, you're against me; if you don't gather with me, you scatter.

---

[10]The argument here is crushing, because they were painfully aware that their "sons" obviously were *not* casting out any devils at all—with *anybody's* help. The implication is that if they are not opposing satanic forces, they must be in league with them, that is, one of them. And since their *sons* are devils, what would one surmise as to the nature of the *fathers?* Since a baby devil, then, is conclusive proof that his pappy is a devil, "your sons shall be the evidence that convicts you."

[11]Relentlessly he drives home his point. By *opposing* evil forces, he has placed himself on God's side and God is supporting him. Therefore, his opponents are now inescapably faced with God's Movement.

24. "When a filthy spirit comes out of a man, it goes through dry places looking for a place to settle down. If it finds none, it says, 'I'll go back to my former home.' So he comes back and finds it all swept and orderly. Then he goes and invites in seven spirits meaner than himself, and they go in and take possession of the place. So the man is much worse off at the end than he was at the beginning."

27. As he was saying these things, a woman in the crowd shouted out, "Praise God for the woman who bore you and at whose breasts you sucked!"

He said, "Instead, praise God for those who listen to God's ideas and put them into practice."

29. When attendance kept increasing, he began by saying, "This is a mean generation. It wants to see 'proof,' and no proof will be given it except Jonah's proof. For just as Jonah became a 'proof' to the Ninevites, even so will the son of man be to this generation. The Queen of the South will be raised up on Judgment Day as convicting evidence against the men of this generation, because she came from the ends of the earth to learn from Solomon's wisdom, and now a greater one than Solomon is here. The men of Nineveh will be raised up on Judgment Day as convicting evidence against this generation, because they reshaped their lives when Jonah preached to them, and now a greater one than Jonah is here.

33. "A person never lights a lamp and puts it in a closet or under a box. Instead he puts it on a table, so as to provide light for all who come in.

"The body's lamp is your eye. When your eyes are in focus [i.e., on a single object], your whole body is distinctly guided; but when they are crossed [i.e., with one eye on one thing, the other on another, or trying to keep an equal eye on two masters], your body is 'in the dark.' See to it, then, that your 'light' isn't 'night.' For if your whole being is illuminated, without any part

50

reserved for darkness, you'll be as completely lit up as when a flash of lightning shines on you."

37. During the talk, a church member asked him to have lunch with him. When he got there, he sat right down at the table and began eating. When the church member saw that, he was stunned, because Jesus didn't observe the church rules about washing things before eating. So the Master said to him, "Now you church members are careful to keep up the outward show, but your insides are full of greediness and meanness. You dimwits, didn't the same one who made the outside also make the inside? But dedicate your *inner* life as an unreserved gift, and then you are clean in every respect.

42. "But there's hell for you church members, because you scrupulously tithe, while by-passing God's judgment and love. You should have done the former without neglecting the latter. There's hell for you church members, because you love the platform chairs in the sanctuary, and the slap on the back at the club luncheons. Hell for you, because you are like old graves of which there is no longer any evidence, and over which people walk without being aware that anybody's buried there."

45. One of the seminary teachers spoke up and said, "Professor, when you say things like that you insult us too."

He said, "And for you professors, hell. Because you load people up with burdensome doctrines, but you yourselves don't lift a finger to put them into practice. There's hell for you, because you memorialize the men of God whom your predecessors killed for heresy. The fact that they murdered them and you build their monuments is evidence that you are parties to your predecessors' deeds. This is why the 'Wisdom of God' says, 'I will send them men of God and ambassadors, and they will persecute them and kill some of them.'

"This generation will have to account for the blood of all the men of God which has been shed from the beginning of time, from

Abel's blood to the blood of Zachariah, who was shot between the church and the parsonage. I repeat, this generation will have to give an account.

"Hell for you, seminary professors, because you carry the key to spiritual wisdom, but you yourselves don't dare enter, and you even restrain others who would."

53. When he left there, the seminary alumni and church members began to really lay into him and pick his mind, setting traps to catch him in something he said.

12.

1. Now when a crowd gathered, so large that people actually trampled on one another, he began to say to his students:

"First of all, be on your guard against the leaven of the church members, which is hypocrisy. For nothing is concealed that won't be revealed, and nothing secret that won't be found out. What you say in the dark will be heard in the light, and what you whisper in somebody's ear behind closed doors, will be broadcast from the rooftops. I want to tell you, my friends, don't fear those who kill the body and then have nothing further they can do. But I *will* show you whom you may well fear: fear the one who has the power not only to kill your body but to damn your soul. Yes, indeed, fear such a one.

6. "Aren't five baby chicks sold for fifty cents? And yet God never forgets even one of them! Why, he even keeps account of all the hairs on your head! So stop fretting. You are worth more than a whole brooderful of baby chicks.

8. "I tell you, too, if anybody will stand up for me before his fellowmen, I will stand up for him before God's angels. But he who lets me down before his fellowmen, shall be let down before God's angels. And anyone who speaks out openly against the son of man will be forgiven, but he who plays false with the Holy Spirit will not be forgiven.

"And when they try you before church councils and courts and investigating committees, don't get all worked up inside about how you'll defend yourself and what you'll say. The Holy Spirit will give you the right word at the right time."

13. Somebody in the crowd said to him, "Preacher, speak to my brother about dividing the inheritance with me."

Jesus said to him, "Say, fellow, who appointed me as a judge or arbitrator between you two?"

Then he said to them, "You all be careful and stay on your guard against all kinds of greediness. For a person's life is not for the piling up of possessions."[12]

16. He then gave them a Comparison: "A certain rich fellow's farm produced well. And he held a meeting with himself and he said, 'What shall I do? I don't have room enough to store my crops.' Then he said, 'Here's what I'll do: I'll tear down my old barns and build some bigger ones in which I'll store all my wheat and produce. And I will say to myself, 'Self, you've got enough stuff stashed away to do you a long time. Recline, dine, wine, and shine!' But God said to him, 'You nitwit, at this very moment your goods are putting the screws on your soul. All these things you've grubbed for, to whom shall they really belong?' That's the way it is with a man who piles up stuff for himself without giving God a thought "

22. He said to his students, "That's why I'm telling you not to worry about your physical life—what you'll eat—or for your body— what you'll wear. For life is much more than eating, and the body is more than clothing. Take a look at the crows. They don't plant, they don't harvest, they don't store things away in cribs or barns. Yet God cares for *them*. *You* are considerably more valuable than

---

[12]Or, no one enriches his life by increasing his possessions.

birds. Besides, which one of you, by fretting and fuming, can make himself one inch taller? Well, if your worrying can't change a little thing like that, why wear yourself out over anything else?

27. "Now take a look at the lilies, how they do no knitting or sewing; yet I'm telling you that not even Solomon, in all his finery, was ever dressed up like one of them. Well then, if God so outfits a plant that one day is growing in the field and the next is used for fuel, he'll do even more for *you*, you spiritual runts. The people of the world go tearing around after all these things. But your Father knows you need them. So set your heart on his Movement, and such things will be fully supplied.

32. "Stop being so scared, my little flock. *Your Father has decided to make you responsible for the Movement.* Sell what you own and give it with no strings attached. Make yourselves wallets that don't wear out, an unsurpassed spiritual treasure which thieves don't plunder, nor worms consume. For your treasure and your heart are wrapped up together.

35. "Roll out now and put on your pants, and turn on the lights. Be on your toes, like workers expecting the boss back from lunch, and when he comes and looks around, they'll be hard at it. Lucky are those workers who, when the boss slips up on them, are on their jobs. I'm telling you, he'll praise them, lend them a hand, and even invite them to lunch with him. And suppose he comes back after hours and finds them working away, they're really top-notch workers. For you may be sure of this: if a homeowner knew what time the thief was coming, he wouldn't allow his house to be broken into. So you all, be constantly on your toes, because the son of man might come when you're not expecting it."

41. Rock said, "Sir, are you telling this Comparison just to us, or to everybody else, too?"

The Master said, "Well, who is the loyal and efficient employee whom his employer will put in charge of the payroll to see that everyone is promptly and accurately paid? Happy is that worker who, when the boss shows up, is doing a good job. I'm telling you a fact, he'll give him one promotion after another. But if that worker begins to say to himself, 'My boss will be late this morning,' and starts throwing his weight around and abusing those under him, then he goes out to get something to eat and a few beers, sure as everything his boss will show up just when he is least expected, and will chew him out and fire him.

"Now that worker who understands fully what his boss wants done and doesn't get busy and do the job, will have the book thrown at him. But the worker who didn't understand, even though he did what he shouldn't have, will get off light. The more one is given, the more is expected of him; the more somebody is entrusted with, the more he must account for.

49. "I came to kindle a fire on the earth, and what wouldn't I give if it were already roaring! I have an ordeal to go through, and how pressed I am until it comes to a head! Do you all think that I came to give the world peace? No, I tell you, not peace but conflict. From now on, if a house has five people in it, they shall be fighting—three against two and two against three. A father will be against his son, and the son against his father; a mother against her daughter, and the daughter against her mother; a mother-in-law against the bride, and the bride against her mother-in-law."

54. He said to the crowd, "When you see a cloud blowing in from the west, right away you say, 'Here comes a rain,' and sure enough, it does rain. And when the south wind is blowing you say, 'It's gonna be hot,' and hot it is. You phonics, you are skilled at weighing scientific facts, but how is it that you can't interpret the signs of the times? And why can't you tell what's right for you? For example, when you're going to court with a man, wouldn't it be better to make an effort to settle out of court rather than having him drag you before the judge, and the judge rule against you, and deliver you into the custody of the warden, and the warden slap you into the pen? I'm telling you, you won't get out of there till you've paid through the nose."

13.

1. Some of the people present at that time told him about the demonstrators who were killed on their way to church.[13]

He replied to them, "Do you suppose that these particular demonstrators were any worse than all the rest just because they suffered this fate? No, I tell you, but unless you all re-shape your lives, every last one of you will suffer a similar fate. Or those eighteen on whom the building in College Park fell and killed them, do you think this happened to them because they were worse sinners than all the other citizens of Atlanta? No, I tell you, but unless you all re-shape your lives, every last one of you will suffer a similar fate."

6. He gave them this Comparison: "A fellow had a peach tree planted in his orchard, and one day he came looking for some fruit on it but didn't find anything. He said to the hired hand, 'Listen here, for three years I've come looking for some fruit on that peach tree and I haven't found a peach. Chop it down. Why let it take up space? But the hired hand said, 'Sir, let it stay just one more year, and I'll hoe around it and put some manure on it. If it should bear fruit then, okay; if it doesn't, chop it down.' "

10. One Sunday he was teaching in one of the churches. And a woman was there who for eighteen years had had a weak spirit and was so bent down she couldn't look up. When Jesus saw her, he called out and said to her, "Lady, you have been freed from

---

[13]The literal translation is "the Galileans whose blood Pilate mixed with their sacrifices." It is possible that Pilate suspected them of "agitating" against the Roman rule and considered them as using religion as a pious cover-up. He brutally murdered them as they were preparing for worship.

your weakness." He put his hands on her, and right away she was straightened up, and started praising God.

But the pastor of the church, indignant that Jesus had healed her on a Sunday, said to the people, "There are *six days* in which it is all right to work. Come on one of them and get yourselves healed, but *not* on a Sunday."

The Master replied, "You bunch of hypocrites! Doesn't every one of you on Sunday turn his cow or horse out of the stall so it can go drink? All right, now take this fine white lady, who had been spiritually locked up for *eighteen years;* don't you think *she* should have been released from *her* bondage *on Sunday?*"

This kind of argument surely did shake up his enemies, but most of the people were overjoyed at the wonderful things he was doing.

18. Then he said, "What is the God Movement like, and with what shall I compare it? It's like a mustard seed which a man plants in his garden, and it keeps growing until it becomes a big bush, and the birds in the sky make its branches their home."

20. And again he said, "With what shall I compare the God Movement? It's like yeast which a housewife mixes in three cups of flour until it all rises."

22. And he went through cities and villages, teaching and making his way towards Atlanta. Somebody asked him, "Sir, will only a few make the grade?"

He said to them, "Do your best to enter the door of all-out commitment. Many, I tell you, will try to enter but just won't have the strength. It's like the owner of an eating joint who goes and locks up for the night, and all who have been standing around outside will then begin to bang on the door and say, 'Open up and let us in.' And he'll say to you, 'I don't know you guys.' Then you'll start saying, 'We're your pals. We've eaten and drunk here before, and you've met us on the streets.' And he'll answer you, 'No, I don't know you. Now go on away from here, you trouble makers.' Out there, there'll be a lot of cussing and hell-raising when you see Abraham, Isaac, and Jacob, as well as all the faithful preachers, *in* the God Movement, while you are left on the outside. People will come from the east and west, from the north and south, and all will sit down together at the same table in the God Movement. And imagine it, those at the foot shall be at the head, and those at the head shall be at the foot."

31. Just then some church members came to him and said, "You better clear out of here in a hurry, because Governor Herod wants to kill you."

He said to them, "Go tell that sly old fox that today and tomorrow I'm casting out demons and carrying on my healing work. The day after that I'll be finished [in Galilee, Herod's province]. You know, I've got to keep going today, tomorrow and the day after tomorrow, because it just isn't proper for a prophet to get killed outside the state capital.

34. "O Atlanta, Atlanta, you who crush the life out of your men of God, and ostracize those who try to show you a better way, many a time I've wanted to bring your citizens together as a hen gathers her biddies under her wings, and you would have none of it. All right, your city's future is left up to you. But I'll tell you this: you won't see me around again until you're crying out, 'Please, God, send us some dedicated leadership.' "

14.

1. Now it so happened one Sunday that he went home to dinner with one of the denominational leaders, who were keeping a close eye on him. And a man with dropsy was there, so Jesus asked the leaders and church officials, "Is it all right to heal on Sunday or not?" When they buttoned up their lips, he took hold of the man, healed him and sent him on his way.

5. Again he asked them, "Suppose one of you had a child or a cow to fall in a well on a Sunday, wouldn't you try to get it out right away?" They just couldn't answer questions like that.

7. Noting the scramble for the places of honor at the table, he gave some advice to the church leaders who had invited him. "When you are invited by someone to a banquet, don't go immediately to the head table. It might be that some big shot with a higher title than yours has been invited, too, and the person in charge of seating arrangements will have to say to you, 'Please let this gentleman have your seat.' Then with embarrassment you'll begin to step down to the lower seat. But when you're invited, take the most inconspicuous seat, and if the emcee comes in and says to you, 'Hello, my friend. Come on up here,' then you'll feel honored before all the guests. For anyone who promotes himself will be humiliated, and he who humbles himself will be promoted."

12. He had a word, too, for his host. "When you give a luncheon or a dinner, don't invite your close friends or your family or your relatives or your rich neighbors, because they might give *you* a pay-back party and you'll just break even. But when you give any kind of a party, invite the poor, the disabled, the crippled and the blind. It will make you very happy, because they don't have anything with which to pay you back. Yet you'll be amply 'repaid' when the truly good are made to live."

15. When one of those eating at the table with him heard these things, he said, "It's a great privilege to sit down and eat together in the God Movement."

Jesus said to him, "One time a man gave a big dinner, and he sent invitations to many people. When everything was on the table, he sent his servant around to all the guests saying, 'Y'all come, it's all ready.' But one after another began to beg off. The first one said, 'I have bought a tract of land, and I've just got to go look it over. If you will, please excuse me.' And another said, 'I have bought five teams of mules, and I simply must go and try them out. If you will, please excuse me.' Another said, 'I just got married, and therefore I *cannot* come!' So the servant returned and told his boss what had happened. Then the boss had a fit, and said to his servant, 'Run out real quick into the streets and alleys of the city, and bring in here the poor and the disabled and the blind and the crippled.' After a while his servant announced, 'Sir, I've done what you told me, but the table still isn't full.' The boss then said to the servant, 'Well, go out on the highway and sidewalks and collar them to come on in here, so I'll have a full table. Because I'm telling you a fact, not one of those guys who got an invitation will get a taste of my food.' "

25. Quite a crowd was trailing him, and he turned and said to them, "If anyone is considering joining me, and does not break his attachment for father and mother and wife and children and brothers and sisters, indeed—for his own life—he simply cannot belong to my fellowship. Anyone who does not accept his own lynching and fall in behind me cannot belong to my fellowship.

28. "If any of you were intending to put up a building, wouldn't you first sit down and figure out the cost, so you could see if you had enough to finish it? Otherwise, you might lay out the foundation, and because you didn't have funds to go any further, people would begin making cracks about you, saying, 'This fellow is a great hand at starting things, but he can't carry through on them.'

31. "Or suppose a king were going out to battle against another king, wouldn't he first sit down and determine whether or not, with his ten thousand men, he could face an enemy of twenty thousand? If he figures he can't, then while there is still distance between them, he should send a delegation to seek for terms of peace.

"So that's the way it is with you. Everyone of you who doesn't throw in his entire fortune cannot belong to my fellowship.

34. "Salt is a good thing, but if it becomes so diluted that it is no longer salt, how can anything be seasoned with it? It's no good even for the soil or the compost heap. People just throw it away. Now remember that, will you?"

15.

1. Now all the "nigger-lovers" and black people were gathering around him to listen. And the white church people and Sunday school teachers were raising cain, saying, "This fellow associates with black people and *eats* with them." So Jesus gave them this Comparison:

3. "Is there a man among you who, if he has a hundred sheep and loses one of them, will not leave the ninety-nine in the pasture and go hunt for the lost one? And when he finds it, he joyfully puts it on his shoulders and goes home with it. He calls over to his friends and neighbors, 'Hey, y'all, I found my lost sheep. Isn't that wonderful?' I'm telling you, in the same way there'll be more joy among the spiritually sensitive ones over a single 'outsider' who reshapes his life than over the ninety-nine 'righteous' people who don't need to change their ways.

8. "Or suppose a woman has ten dimes and loses one of them; won't she get the flashlight and a broom and sweep and look carefully till she finds it? And when she does find it, she calls over to her friends and neighbors and says, 'Hey, y'all, you know that dime I lost? Well, I found it. Isn't that nice?' In the same way, I tell you, there's a rejoicing on the part of God's faithful ones over a single 'outsider' who re-shapes his life."

11. He went on to say, "A man had two sons. The younger one said to his father, 'Dad, give me my share of the business.' So he split up the business between them. Not so long after that the younger one packed up all his stuff and took off for a foreign land, where he threw his money away living like a fool. Soon he ran out of cash, and on top of that, the country was in a deep depression. So he was really hard up. He finally landed a job with one of the citizens of that country, who sent him into the fields to feed *hogs!* And he was hungry enough to tank up on the slop the hogs were eating. Nobody was giving him even a hand-out.

"One day an idea bowled him over. 'A lot of my father's hired hands have more than enough bread to eat, and out here I'm starving in this depression. I'm gonna get up and go to my father and say, 'Dad, I've sinned against God and you, and am no longer fit to be called your son—just make me one of your hired hands.'

"So he got up and came to his father. While he was some distance down the road, his father saw him and was moved to tears. He ran to him and hugged him and kissed him and kissed him.

"The boy said, 'Dad, I've sinned against God and you, and I'm not fit to be your son any more—' But the father said to his servants, 'You all run quick and get the best suit you can find and put it on him. Get his family ring for his hand and some dress shoes for his feet. Then I want you to bring that stall-fed steer and butcher it, and let's all eat and whoop it up, because this son of mine was given up for dead, and he's still alive; he was lost and is now found.' And they began to whoop it up.

"But his older son was out in the field. When he came in and got almost home, he heard the music and the dancing, and he called one of the little boys and asked him what in the world was going on. The little boy said, 'Why, your brother has come home, and your daddy has butchered the stall-fed steer, because he got him back safe and sound. At this he blew his top, and wouldn't go in. His father went out and pleaded with him. But he answered his father, 'Look here, all these years I've slaved for you, and never once went contrary to your orders. And yet, at no time have you ever given me so much as a baby goat with which to pitch a party for my friends. But when this son of yours—who has squandered the business on whores—comes home, you butcher for him the stall-fed steer.' But he said to him, 'My boy, my dear boy, you are with me all the time, and what's mine is yours. But I just can't *help* getting happy and whooping it up, because *this brother of yours* was dead and is alive; he was lost and has been found.' "

16.

1. He said to his students, "Once there was a rich man who hired a manager for his business. Later he got wind that his manager was making a mess of things. So he called him in the office and said, 'What's this I'm hearing about you? Let me have your accounts, so I can see if you can be manager around here any longer.'

"The manager went out and thought it over. 'What shall I do, seeing as how my boss is taking my job away from me? I'm not able to do physical labor, and I'm ashamed to go on welfare . . . I've got it! I'll fix it so that when I'm fired as manager they'll still welcome me into their places of business.' So he called up each one of his boss's customers and said to the first one, 'How much do you owe my boss?' He replied, 'I owe him for 900 gallons of oil.' 'All right,' said the manager, 'we'll settle the account if you'll sit right down and write us a check for 450 gallons. Okay?' Then he said to another, 'And you, how much do you owe?' He replied, 'For 1000 bushels of wheat.' The manager said, 'Just write us a check for 800 in full settlement.'

"And the boss gave the crooked manager·*credit* for pulling such a slick trick.

"You know, pagan business men are smarter than Christians in conducting their affairs. So I'm telling you, get yourselves some friends among the money boys so that when you fall flat on your face they might invite you into their plush offices (to give you some advice)!

10. "Anybody who is honest in small matters will be honest in important affairs, and he who is crooked in small details will be crooked in larger matters. So if you don't know how to handle money matters, who'll entrust to you real wealth? And if you don't take care of what belongs to somebody else, how do you expect to have anything of your own?

"No worker can hire out to two bosses at the same time. For either he will have contempt for one and respect for the other, or he will look up to one and down on the other. You absolutely cannot be loyal to both God and Money."

14. Now the money-loving church members heard all this, and started booing him. He said to them, "You people make yourselves look pretty in public, but God knows your hearts. And what men praise, God abhors.

16. "Until John, men were faced with the law and the prophets. Since then, the news of the God Movement is being circulated, and everyone is being forced to face it.

"It's easier for land and sky to pass away than for one crossing of a 't' to fall away from the law.

18. "Anyone who divorces his wife and marries another is having illicit sex relations, and the divorced wife who remarries has illicit sex relations.

19. "Once there was a rich man, and he put on his tux and stiff shirt, and staged a big affair every day. And there was laid at his gate a poor guy by the name of Lazarus, full of sores, and so hungry he wanted to fill up on the rich man's table scraps. On top of this, the dogs came and licked his sores.

"It so happened that the poor fellow died, and the angels seated him at the table with Abraham. The rich man died, too, and was buried. And in the hereafter, the rich man, in great agony, looked up and saw from afar Abraham, and Lazarus sitting beside him at the table. So he shouted to him, 'Mr. Abraham, please take pity on me and send Lazarus to dip the end of his finger in some water and rub it over my tongue, because I'm scorching in this heat.'

"Abraham replied, 'Boy, you remember that while you were alive you got the good things (the good jobs, schools, streets, houses, etc.), while at the same time Lazarus got the left-overs. But now, here *he's* got it made, and you're scorching. And on top of all this, somebody has dug a yawning chasm between us and you, so that people trying to get through from here to you can't make it, neither can they get through from there to us.'

"The rich man said, 'Well, then, Mr. Abraham, will you please send him to my father's house, for I have five brothers; let him thoroughly warn them so they won't come to this hellish condition.'

"Then Abraham said, 'They've got the Bible and the preachers; let them listen to them.'

"But he said, 'No, they won't do that, Mr. Abraham. But if somebody will go to them from the dead, they'll change their ways!'

"He replied, 'Well, if they won't listen to the Bible and the preachers, they won't be persuaded even if someone does get up from the dead.'"

17.

1. Then he said to his students, "It is unlikely that there won't be any traps, but hell to him who sets them. He would be better off pitched into the sea with a grinding rock draped around his neck, than to set a trap for one of these little ones. Keep an eye on yourselves.

"If your brother does you wrong, face him up to it. And if he apologizes and acts differently, let him off. Even if he does you wrong seven times a day, and seven times a day turns to you and says, 'I'm sorry. I'll do better,' you must let him off."

5. The students said to the Master, "Step up our faith."

And the Master said, "Why, if you have the faith of a mustard seed, you could say to this pecan tree, 'Uproot yourself and plant yourself in the lake,' and it would do as you say.

7. "Suppose one of you has a servant chopping cotton or feeding chickens. When she comes to the house that night, would you say to her, 'Come on and let's eat'? No indeed! You would say to her, 'Wash up and get supper for me, and wait on me while I'm eating and drinking, and when I get through then you can have your supper.' Does one *thank* a servant for merely doing what he is told? All right, that's the way it is with you. When you've done what you've been told, you should say ,'We're but undeserving servants doing our duty.' "

11. While he was on his way to Atlanta, he went through the ghetto of Griffin, where he was met by ten winos who stood at a distance and yelled, "Mister Jesus, have mercy on us!" When he saw them he said, "Okay, go show yourselves to the doctor." And as they were going, they were cured. Now one of them, realizing that he was cured, turned around and shouted at the top of his voice, "Praise God! Praise God!" Then he got down before Jesus and thanked him. This particular one was a black man. So Jesus said, "Weren't there ten of you that got healed? Where are the other nine? Well, well. So didn't any of them come back here to praise and thank God except this black man, huh?"

He said to the man, "Get up and go. Your trustful action has been the making of you."

20. Some of the church members asked him when the God Movement would get up steam. He answered them, "The God Movement doesn't get up steam by appointing a committee to study it. Nor can you say, 'It's here' or 'It's there,' for evidences of the God Movement are all about you."

22. Then he said to his students, "The time will come when you'd give anything to re-live one of these days with me, but you won't be able. And they'll tell you, 'Look, there he is,' or 'Look, here he is.' Don't get excited and go running out. For at that time my presence among you will be like a bolt of lightning flashing from one end of the sky to the other. But first, I've got to suffer a lot, and to be run off by the general public. My presence here will be just like it was in the days when Noah confronted the people. They went their merry way of eating, drinking, marrying, courting, until the very day Noah went into the ark and the flood came and drowned them all. Or like it was at the time of Lot. They went merrily on their way, eating, drinking, buying, selling, planting, building, until the very day Lot left Sodom, and it rained fire and brimstone from the sky and destroyed them all. That's exactly the way it'll turn out on the day the son of man confronts people. When *that* happens, don't let the man sitting on the porch try to save his furniture, or the man in the field hold on to his hoe. *Remember what happened to Lot's wife!* If anyone tries to take precautions for his life, he'll lose it, and if anyone turns it loose, he'll burst into blossom. I'm telling you, on that night of confrontation, two brothers will be sleeping in the same bed; the one will be caught up by it and the other will be left snoring. Two sisters will be getting dinner together; the one will be caught up by it and the other will be left cooking."

Their response was, "*Where*, sir?"

He replied, "Where there's a dead body, there, too, will the buzzards be gathered."

18.

1. He told them a Comparison to show that they should keep on praying and not give up. "One time in a certain city there was a judge who didn't believe in God, and didn't give a hoot about people. In the same city was a widow, and she came to him repeatedly and said, 'Please, hear my case against so-and-so.' He put her off for a long time, but finally he said to himself: 'Even though I don't believe in God and don't give a hoot for people, yet because this woman has got it in for me, I'll hear her case before she finally nags me to death.' "

6. The Master said, "Listen to what this wicked judge is saying. How much more readily will *God* have compassion on and hear the case of his special workers who are in contact with him night and day! I tell you, he'll hear their case at once. *But*, will the son of man find *faith* on the earth when he confronts it?"

9. Also, he gave this Comparison to certain ones who had a high regard for their own goodness, but looked down their noses at others: "Two men went into the chapel to pray. The one was a church member, the other was an unsaved man. The church member stood up and prayed to himself like this: 'O God, I thank you that I'm not like other people—greedy, mean, promiscuous— or even like this unsaved man. *I* go to church *twice* on Sunday, and *I* am a faithful *tither* of all my income.' But the unsaved man, standing way off, wouldn't even lift up his eyes, but knelt down and cried, 'O God, have mercy on a sinner like me.' I'm telling you, this man went home cleaned up rather than that one. For everyone who puts *himself* on a pedestal will be laid low, and everyone who lays himself low will be put on a pedestal."

15. Some folks started bringing their babies to him to bless, and his students jumped on them for it. Jesus then gathered the little ones around him and said, "Let the kids come to me and don't get in their way, for of such is the God Movement. I truly tell you that unless one accepts the God Movement like a child, he just won't get into it."

18. One of the leading citizens asked him, "Good Doctor, what do I do to come into possession of spiritual life?"

Jesus replied, "Why do you call me 'good'? You know the commandments—don't sleep with someone you're not married to, don't murder, don't steal, don't lie, take care of your father and mother."

But he said, "I know, and I've observed these ever since I was a youngster."

When Jesus heard that, he said, "You're falling short in one thing: Sell all you've got, give it to the poor—you'll be spiritually rich—and come share my life."

When he heard all this, the man was heart-broken, because he was powerfully rich.

Jesus looked at him and said, "How terribly difficult it is for those who own things to come into the God Movement. Actually it's easier to thread a needle with a rope than for a rich man to get into the God Movement."

Those listening said, "Well, *who* then can be saved?"

"Things humanly impossible," he said, "are possible with God."

Rock spoke up, "Gee, look at *us! We* have given up all we owned and have shared your life."

Jesus said to them, "I surely tell you all, there is no one who has given up a house or a wife or brothers or parents or children, for the God Movement, who will not receive all of these many times over right here and now, and—in the approaching era—spiritual life."

31. He called the twelve aside and said to them. "Look, we're going up to Atlanta, and everything the old-time men of God wrote about the son of man is going to happen. He will be handed over to the people of the world and shall be made fun of and insulted and spit on. They'll beat him up and kill him, but on the third day he'll be raised up."

But they didn't understand a thing he said. It was all too deep for them, so they didn't catch on to what he was talking about.

35. When he got near Hampton, a blind man was sitting on the street begging. He heard the noise of the crowd and asked somebody what in the world was going on. They told him that Jesus of Valdosta was passing through. He yelled as loud as he could, "Jesus, King Jesus, have mercy on me." The people up front told him to cut it out and keep quiet. But he shouted all the louder, "King Jesus, have mercy on me." Jesus stopped and ordered him to be brought to him. When he got there, Jesus inquired, "What can I do for you?"

He said, "Mister, I want to *see*."

Jesus said to him, "Okay, SEE! Your faith has been the making of you."

And right away he could *see*, and he was running around praising God. The whole crowd saw it and started praising God, too.

19.

1. He entered and passed on through Hampton. Now a man was there by the name of Zeke Geers. He was district director of the Revenue Service, and was quite well off. He was trying to get a glimpse of Jesus to see what he looked like, but he couldn't do it because of the crowd, and because he was a short man.

So he ran on ahead and climbed up a pecan tree so he could spot him, because Jesus was about to pass that way. When Jesus got to the place, he looked up and said to him, "Zeke Geers, hurry up and come down, because I need to stay at your house today." Mr. Geers slid down right away and gladly took him home with him.

When the good white people saw this, they grumbled, "He's going home to dinner with a man who doesn't even belong to the church."

During the meal, Mr. Geers got up and said to the Master, "Look, half of what I own, sir, I'm giving to the poor, and if I have . . . er . . . cheated anyone . . . er . . . anyone, that is. I'll pay back *four* times the amount."

Jesus said to him, "Today new life has arrived at *this* house! Because after all, he, too, is a white man, and the son of man came to search out and rescue *anybody* who gets off the track."

11. While they were pondering on these things, he added a Comparison. He told this one because he was near Atlanta, and because they were thinking that the God Movement was about to burst forth immediately. Therefore he said: "A man from one of the best families went to a distant city to receive his appointment as Governor General and then return to his province. Before he left, he called ten of his workers and turned over to them ten thousand dollars with this instruction: 'You all do business till I get back.'

"Some politicians couldn't stand him, so they sent a committee to follow him and say, 'We don't want this fellow for our Governor General.'

"Now when he returned with his appointment as Governor, he called up the workers to whom he had given the money so as to find out who had gained what. The first one came up and said, 'Sir, your money has increased ten times.'

"And he said to him, 'That's fine. You are a good worker. Because you have done a good job with this small amount, you may have charge of ten cities.'

"The second one came and said, 'The money you gave me, sir, has increased five times.'

"And he said to this one, 'All right, you can be over five cities.'

"Another one came and said, 'Look, sir, here's your money, which I've tied up in a bandanna. For I was scared of you, since you're a very hard-hearted man. You demand what you never deposited, and you harvest what you never planted.'

"He said to him, 'I'll use your own words to judge you, you good-for-nothing bum! You say that I'm a hard-hearted man, demanding what I don't deposit and harvesting what I don't plant. All right, then, why didn't you let the banker have my money so that when I got back I might at least have had the interest?' Then he said

71

to the attendants, 'Take the money from him and give it to the first man.' They said to him, 'But sir, he has ten thousand already.'

" 'And as for those enemies of mine who didn't want me to be their Governor, bring them here and destroy them before me.'

"I tell you, responsibility will be given to everyone who will exercise it, and from him who won't, even what responsibility he has will be taken away."

28. After saying this, he moved on toward Atlanta. When he got near Jonesboro, near a hill called "The Peach Orchard," he sent two of his students, telling them, "Go into the town ahead, and there you'll find a young mule tied up, which has never been broke for riding. Untie him and bring him here. And if anyone asks you, 'Why are you untying him?', you say, 'His owner needs him.' "

So they went and found everything just as he had told them. And while they were untying the young mule, his owners said to them, "Why are you untying the mule?" And they said, "Because his owner needs him."

35. They brought him to Jesus, took off their shirts and laid them on the mule, and then mounted Jesus on him. While he was moving along, people were spreading their clothes in the road. When he arrived at "Peach Orchard" hill, a big crowd of his followers got happy and started shouting, "Praise God for the miracles we've seen!" Then they sang,

"Hail to the Chief, who comes with the name of 'Lord'!
Heavenly Peace and highest Praise!"

Some of the church members in the crowd said to him, "Doctor, tell your followers to restrain themselves."

"I tell you," he said, "if they fall silent, the *rocks* will break into song."

41. And as he drew near and saw the skyline of the city, he burst into tears over it, saying, "Oh, if you had just known at this time the things which lead to peace! Even now they don't make sense to you. The days will come when your enemies will throw up fortifications around you, and besiege you, and take you prisoner, and sack you and your inhabitants, and not leave one building standing, simply because you didn't recognize your day of opportunity."

And he went into the First Church, and began turning out the money-raisers, telling them, "The Scripture says, 'My house is a house for prayer,' but you all have made it a bankers' club."

He was teaching every day in the church. But the bishops and theologians and key leaders were trying to destroy him. Yet they found no way to get at him, because the people were hanging around listening to him.

20.

1. It so happened on one of the days while he was teaching and explaining the God Movement to the people in the church, that the bishops and professors, along with the church officials, laid into him and said, "Tell us where you got the authority to do such things. Who gave you this permission?"

3. He replied, "Let me ask *you* a question and I want you to answer me. Was John's baptism divine or human?"

They conferred with one another, saying, "If we say it is divine, he will ask why we didn't accept it. If we say it is human, the crowd will mob us, because they're convinced that John is a man of God."

So they answered that they didn't know which it was.

Jesus said to them, "Well, then, I won't tell you where I got the authority for my actions."

9. Then he began telling the people this Comparison: "A man set out a peach orchard, turned it over to some sharecroppers and went on a long trip. When the peaches got ripe, he sent his assistant to look after his share of the crop. But the croppers beat him up and ran him off empty-handed. He sent still another assistant, and they beat him up, too, and cussed him out and ran him off empty-handed. So he sent a third one, and him, too, they clubbed and dragged out.

"The owner of the orchard said, 'What shall I do? Perhaps if I send my son, who is so dear to me, they'll surely have respect for him.'

"But when the croppers saw him, they said to one another, 'Look, this is the old man's heir. Let's kill him, and the orchard might fall to us by squatters' rights.' So they dragged him outside the orchard and killed him.

"Now what will the owner of the peach orchard do to them? He'll come himself and destroy those croppers and rent his orchard to someone else."

They who heard this said, "Good God, no!"

He looked them over and said, "What then does this Scripture mean: 'The stone which the builders turned down, has turned up as the keystone in the structure'? Anyone who falls on *that* stone will be shattered, but whomever *it* falls on will be utterly smashed."

19. Now the seminary professors and denominational executives tried to lay hands on him right then and there, but were afraid of their constituency. For they knew full well that he had aimed this Comparison at them. So they played it cool by hiring some detectives to pose as Christians and collect evidence from his preaching, so he could be arrested and turned over to the House Subversive Activities Committee. These detectives asked him, "Doctor, we know when *you* speak and teach you shoot straight, regardless of who's listening. We know, too, that beyond any doubt you are teaching God's Way. Now, is it right to pay Federal taxes or not?"

Catching on to their trick, he said, "Show me a dollar. Whose picture and insignia is on it?"

They said, "The President's."

He replied, "All right, then, give government things to the government, and God's things to God."

So they were not successful in trapping him in anything he said in public, and his answer so astounded them that they shut up.

27. Then some Humanists, who deny that there is a life hereafter, put this question to him: "Doctor, the Old Testament says that if a married man dies without having any children, his brother should try to have children by the widow so as to provide heirs for his brother. So, there were seven brothers. The first one married and died childless. The second one then took her and then the third, etc., until all seven had lived with her without having children. They all died, and finally the woman died too. Now then, that woman in the life hereafter—whose wife does she become, since all seven were married to her?"

34. Jesus answered them, "People in this life marry and get married, but those who are considered candidates for the next life, and for the raising of the dead, neither marry nor get married. Being immortal, they are like the angels, and being resurrected souls they are God's people.

"But now about the dead being raised, even Moses proved it when—at the burning bush—he calls the Lord 'the God of Abraham and the God of Isaac and the God of Jacob.' He is not, then, a God of the dead but of the living. For *all* draw their life from him."

Some of the seminary professors responded, "Doctor, that was a mag-ni-fi-cent answer!"

After that, nobody felt like asking him *anything*.

41. So he asked them a question. "Why is it said that the Leader of the revolution is to be a descendant of David, when David himself says in the book of Psalms:

'God said to my Lord, "Sit at my right hand until I bring all
  your opponents under your rule." '

75

"If David refers to him as 'Lord,' how can he be his descendant?"

45. While the whole crowd was listening, he said to his students, "Keep away from those religious leaders who insist on wearing academic robes and who love the back-slapping at the civic clubs and the center chairs in the pulpits and the speakers' tables at banquets; who eat widows out of house and home, and make long prayers at the drop of a hat. These will get the Judgment book thrown at them."

21.

1. He looked around and saw the rich folks putting their money into the collection plates. He noticed that a penniless widow put in two cents, and he said, "It is surely true that this poverty-stricken widow put in more than the others, because all of them gave from their overflow, while she, from her scarcity, has put in all she has."

5. Some people were commenting about the First Church, its architecture and the beautiful marble and the stained glass memorial windows.

He said, "All that you're admiring, the time will come when not one piece of marble will be left upon another without being torn down."

"Doctor," they asked, "when will this happen? And how are we to know when all this is ready to take place?"

"Don't let anybody kid you," he replied, "for there will be many people buzzing around calling themselves Christians and preaching, 'I've got the answer,' and 'the time is up.' Don't go trekking after them. Even when you hear reports of fights and factions, don't get alarmed. For these things will of necessity come first, but the end does not immediately follow."

10. Then he continued, "Race will rise against race, and nation against nation. There will be great shake-ups in various places, and there'll be starvation and epidemics. Great, frightful omens will appear in the sky. But before all this happens they'll lay hands on you and arrest you, turning you over to church councils and putting you in jail, and dragging you before courts and committees because you bear my name. It'll turn out to be your opportunity to make a witness. So don't get it in your heads that you've got to prepare your defense in advance. For I'll give to you a mouth and a mind which all your opponents won't be able to match or reply to.

"You'll be turned in even by parents and brothers and relatives and friends, and they'll kill some of you. You'll be hated by everybody because you bear my name. But you won't be really harmed in the slightest. By your uncompromising stand you'll find a new dimension to life.

20. "Now when you see the capital taken over by the military, you'll know that her time is running out. Then let the people in the country run to the hills, and let those in the city itself get out, and those on the farms not enter it. For these are the days of reckoning that so much has been written about. It'll be terrible for the pregnant and the nursing mothers at that time. Throughout the land there'll be nothing but hard times and fury for the people. For they'll be butchered and enslaved by other races, and the nation will be buried under racial problems until all races have full opportunities. And there'll be signals on the sun and moon and stars, and throughout the land there'll be a tension of races in confusion like the roaring of the boiling sea, with men passing out from fear and anticipation of what's happening to civilization. For the powers of the higher-ups will be shaken. And then they'll see the son of man leading a Movement with great strength and authority. When these preliminary things happen, hold up your heads and throw back your shoulders, because your freedom is arriving."

29. And he told them a Comparison: "Take a look at the pear tree and all the other trees. When they are far advanced, you can look and see for yourself that warm weather is here. Likewise, when you all see things like these happening, you can know that the God Movement is here. I truly tell you that the present generation will not be gone before all these things happen. Land and sky will pass away, but what I'm telling you won't. Check up on yourselves to see that your sensitivity isn't dulled by fast living and drunkenness and worry over making a living. Otherwise, the times might catch you suddenly like a trap, for they'll confront everybody in the world. So stay on your toes all the time, praying that you'll have the strength to break loose from that situation and to stand up and be counted for the son of man."

37. During the day he was teaching at First Church, but he would go out and spend the nights at "Peach Orchard Hill." And all the people got up early to hear him speak at the church.

22.

1. Now the annual meeting, which is called the Convention, was drawing near. And the denominational executives and secretaries were trying to find a way to get rid of him, for they didn't trust the people. Then the devil got into Judas Iscariot, who was one of the inner circle of twelve, and he went and discussed with the executives and detectives as to how he might turn Jesus over to them. They were real happy, and offered to pay him money. He agreed, and started looking for an opportunity to turn him over to them apart from the crowd.

7. Then the time came for what the program called "Alumni Banquets and Communion." So he sent Rock and Jack with these instructions: "Go and make arrangements for us to have a banquet." They asked, "Where do you suggest we have it?" He replied, "Well, as you enter the city you'll meet a man carrying a pitcher of ice water. Follow him into the hotel that he enters, and tell the hotel manager, 'The Professor says to ask you, "Where is the dining room where I'm to hold a banquet with my students?" ' He'll show you a large room on the mezzanine. Get it in shape."

They went and found it exactly as he had said, and they got everything ready for the banquet.

14. When the hour arrived, he and the twelve sat down, and he said to them, "With a deep longing I've wanted to eat this annual fellowship meal with you before I suffer. For I'm telling you that I'll not eat it again until it has become a symbol of the God Movement."

And he took a cup, and having given thanks, he said, "Take this and share it among you. I tell you, from now on I'm not drinking 'fruit of the vine' until the God Movement has come."

And he took a loaf, and having given thanks, he broke it and gave it to them, saying, "This is my body.

"But even so, the man who'll turn me in is eating my food. Indeed, the son of man is going his predetermined way, but it will be hell for that fellow who turns him in."

And they began questioning among themselves as to which one of them might do such a thing.

24. Later they got into an argument over who was the most important. He said to them, "Big business men hold the reins over their subordinates, and those invested with authority are called 'executives.' But don't you all act that way. Instead, let the oldest among you be the same as the youngest, and the boss the same as the janitor. Now look, who's the greater, the one eating at the table or the one serving the table? The one eating, of course. But *I'm* taking the position of your *servant*. And you, you're the ones who have shared so deeply with me in my struggles. Now I'm outlining the Movement for you just as my Father outlined it for me, so that you can be my intimate associates in my Movement. And you'll be the twelve pillars of a new 'Reformation.'

31. "Simon! Simon! Look here! Satan begged to run all of you through the combine like heads of wheat. But I prayed over *you* particularly, that your faith might not cave in. And you, when you have got on your feet, help your brothers to stand up."

"Master," he replied, "I am ready to go with you to jail or death."

Jesus said to him, "Rock, I tell you that before the rooster crows at dawn, you'll have denied three times that you ever knew me."

35. He turned to them all. "When I sent you out without a wallet or a suitcase or walking shoes, did you lack for anything?" They said, "Not a thing."

He said, "Okay, but *now* if you've got a wallet, go get it; and do the same if you have a suitcase. If you don't have either, sell your shirt and buy a switchblade. The fact is that it's going to happen to me just as this Scripture says: 'And he was lumped with the lawless.' And it's just about here."

"Master, look here," they said. "We got *two* switchblades."

He said, "Forget it."

39. So he left, and as he had been in the habit of doing, he went out to "Peach Orchard Hill." His students, too, went along. When they got there, he said, "Pray hard that *you* don't get in a bind."

He withdrew from them about a stone's throw and got down on his knees and prayed, "O Father, if you please, relieve me of this agony. But let your wish, rather than mine, be carried out."

(It seemed that an angel from heaven was strengthening him. And being in agony, he prayed the more fervently, and the sweat was pouring from him and on to the ground like blood from a fresh cut.)

And he got up from praying and came to his students, only to find them sleeping from their grief. He said to them, "Why are you sleeping? Get up and start praying so that *you* might not get in a bind."[14]

47. Even as he was speaking, here comes a crowd, and the fellow named Judas, one of the twelve, was leading them. And he came up to Jesus to kiss him. Jesus said to him, "Judas, are you kissing the son of man goodbye?"

When those around him caught on to what would follow, they asked, "Master, shall we slash 'em with the switchblade?" And one of them slashed the bishop's lackey and chopped off his right ear. "Stop it!" shouted Jesus, and he touched the ear and healed it.

He then said to the executives and church workers and officers who had come out to get him, "So you've come out with guns and clubs as though you were after a traitor? Every day I was at the church with you, and you didn't lay hands on me. But this hour when darkness rules, suits you."

54. They grabbed him, took him away, and brought him into the archbishop's house.

Now Rock was trailing a good way behind. When they got a fire going in the backyard and had gathered around it, Rock sidled up, too. A teen-age girl, catching a glimpse of his face in the light, started at him and said, "Hey, this fellow was with him." But he denied it and said, "No, I don't know him, miss."

A little while later someone else saw him and said, "You over there, you were one of them."

Rock said, "Not me, mister."

About another hour passed and a man really jumped him and said, "I know positively this guy was with him, because he sounds like a Yankee."

---

[14]The Greek word for temptation means a testing, a trial, an experiment, a proving of someone of something; thus, to be subjected to unusual pressures, to "get in a bind." Perhaps Jesus is thinking of Judas, who at this moment is on the horns of a dilemma, tormented and pressured by his dual loyalty to Christ the Lord and to Caiaphas the high priest. The other disciples are warned not to let themselves get into a similar predicament.

Rock said to him, "Listen here, man, I don't know what you're talking about."

Right away, while he was saying it, the rooster crowed.

The Master turned and looked at Rock, and Rock recalled the Master's word when he told him, "Before the rooster crows at dawn, you will have denied me three times." And he walked away, and cried like a baby.

63. And the men were shoving Jesus around and poking fun at him and slapping him. They blindfolded him and jeeringly asked, "Guess who socked you?" And many other insults they heaped upon him.

66. When day came, a "peoples' presbytery," composed of executives and professors, met and had him brought into the meeting room. They said, "If you are the Leader, tell us."

"When I tell you something," he answered, "you don't accept it, and when I ask you a question, you don't answer. From here on out, the son of man will be backed up by God's power."

They all said, "Well, then, does that mean you are God's Son?"

He replied, "It does indeed."

They said, "Do we need any further evidence? We ourselves have heard it straight from his own mouth."

23.

1. Then the whole crowd of them got up and took him to Governor Pilate. They began by leveling these charges against him:

"1. We have caught this fellow agitating our people.

2. He advocates the refusal to pay Federal taxes.

3. He claims to be the Leader of a Movement."

Pilate then asked him, "You, are the Head of the Church?"

He answered him, "Yes, I am."

Pilate said to both the church executives and the people, "I don't find this man guilty of anything."

But they kept shouting and yelling, "He's agitating the people, spreading his ideas through the whole state of Georgia, all the way from Alabama to here."

6. When Pilate heard this, he asked if the man had ever lived in Alabama. On learning that he had been in Governor Herod's state, he sent him to Herod, who happened to be in Atlanta on that very day. When Governor Herod saw Jesus he was quite happy, because he had been hearing about him for a long time and had been wanting to see him. He thought he could get him to perform some miracle. He asked Jesus a lot of questions, but he never would answer him. The executives and leading ministers tore into him with all kinds of accusations. Governor Herod and his henchmen made wisecracks and poked fun at him, and finally dressed him up like a big politician and sent him back to Pilate. (From that day on, Herod and Pilate became friends with one another, although previously they had been at each other's throats.)

13. Then Pilate called together the executives and the leaders and the people, and said to them, "You brought this man before me as a rabble-rouser. Now look, I've heard the case publicly, and haven't found this man guilty of a thing that you're accusing him of. Nor did Herod, for he sent him back to us. Clearly he has done nothing to deserve death. So I'm going to whip him and let him go."

18. Howling like a mob, they said, "Do away with this guy! We want 'Daddy-boy'!" (This was a fellow who had been put in jail for inciting to riot in the city and for murder.)

Again Pilate addressed them, wanting to release Jesus. But they yelled back, "Kill him. Kill him."

The third time he said to them, "Why? What's his crime? I've found no reason to give him the death penalty. So I'm going to whip him and let him go."

But they screamed at the top of their voices, demanding that he be killed.

And their voices won.

Pilate decided to grant their request.

He released the one who had been put in jail for riot and murder, just as they asked, and he let them have Jesus to do to him as they pleased.

And so they led him away.

26. Along the road they grabbed Simon "the New Yorker" as he was coming in from the field. They made him walk behind Jesus and tote his cross.

27. There was a big crowd of people following him. There were some women who were sobbing and crying their hearts out over him. Jesus turned and said to them, "Dear sisters of the South, you need not cry over me. Rather, you should cry for yourselves and for your children. Because the time is surely coming when women will say, 'We wish we had been barren and never had a baby or ever nursed a child.' People will then begin to cry out to the mountains, 'Fall on us,' and to the hills, 'Cover us.' Because if they do things like this with green wood, what will they do with dry?"

32. The two other criminals were taken out with him to be killed. And when they came to a place called "Skull," there they killed him and the criminals, the one on his right and the other on his left.

Jesus said, "Father forgive them, for they don't know what they're up to."

They rolled dice to see who would get his clothes.

The crowd stood around staring.

The leaders thumbed their noses at him. They said, "He saved others; let him save himself, if he is really God's special Leader."

The policemen, too, made fun of him. They offered him a drink of whiskey. They said, "Since you are the Head of the Church, save *yourself*."

39. One of the criminals hanging beside him railed at him, "Hey, you, ain't you the Leader? Save yourself and *us*."

But the other one rebuked him. He said, "Ain't you got no fear of God, seeing as how you're accused of the same thing he is? And we had it comin' to us, and got just what we deserved for what we done. But him, he ain't broke no law."

And he said, "Please, Jesus, remember me when you git your Movement goin'."

He said to him, "I tell you straight, today you'll be with me in highest Heaven."

44. It was already about noon. The sun's light went out and darkness settled over the land until three o'clock.

The big curtain in the sanctuary was split in two.

And calling out with a loud cry, Jesus said, "O Father, I'm placing my spirit in your hands." He said this and he died.

Now the police captain, when he saw how it had happened, praised God and said, "Surely this was a good man!"

The whole crowd, who had come along for the sight, when they saw how it all turned out, went home heaving great sobs.

And the people who had known him, with the women who had followed him all the way from Alabama, stood off in the distance to see what was going on.

50. And now, there was a man by the name of Joseph from the white suburb of Sylvan Hills. He was a member of the denominational board, and a good and honest man. (He himself had not voted for their plan of action. In fact, he was a God Movement sympathizer.) This man went to Governor Pilate and requested the body of Jesus. It was granted, and he took down the body and wrapped it in a sheet. Then he put it in a burial vault carved from the rock and in which no one had ever been buried.

It was late Friday afternoon. In just a little while it would be the Sabbath.

The women who had come along with Jesus from Alabama went

with Joseph and saw the vault and how the body was placed in it. Then they went home and fixed some wreaths and potted plants. They kept quiet on the Sabbath, like the Bible said they should.

24.

1. But reàl early on the first day of the week, they came to the vault, bringing the flowers which they had fixed. They found the entrance stone rolled away from the vault, and when they entered they didn't find the body of the Lord Jesus. While they were wondering about this, two men in sparkling clothes stood before them. The women were very much frightened and turned their faces toward the ground. The men said to them, "Why are you looking for a live person among dead ones? Remember how he told you while he was still with you in Alabama that it would be necessary for the son of man to be abandoned into hands of unsympathetic people, and to be lynched, and on the third day to rise?"

They did remember his words. They returned from the vault and told the whole story to the eleven and the rest. The women who were telling the apostles these things were Maria, "the Magdala girl," and Jo Ann and Maria James, and others with them. But it all seemed to the men like so much female chatter, and they wouldn't believe it.

13. But then on that same day, two of them were walking along the road toward a town named Austell, which is seventeen miles from Atlanta. They were talking with one another about all these recent events. While they were talking and raising questions, Jesus himself drew near and joined them. They didn't notice him closely and didn't recognize him. He said to them, "What's all this you're discussing as you walk?"

They just stood there with tears in their eyes. One of them named Clifford said to him, "Are you the only fellow from Atlanta who doesn't know about the things that have been happening there the last few days?"

He said, "What things?"

They said, "Why, about Jesus the Valdostan, a powerful preacher both in his messages from God and in his public actions; how our leading ministers and officials got him a death sentence and killed him. And *we* were hoping all along he'd be the one who would get the church out of its mess. It has now been three days since he was killed.

"But you know, some of our women amazed us. Early this morning they went to the burial vault and didn't find his body. They came back and said they'd had a vision—had seen some angels who told them he was alive! Some of the rest of us went with them to the vault and found it just as the women had said, but we didn't see *him*."

He said to them, "O how dense you are, and how sluggish your minds are in catching on to all that the prophets spoke! Can't you see how necessary it was for the Leader to suffer like this in order to be inaugurated Head?"[15]

28. Then beginning with Genesis and continuing on through the prophets, he explained to them various scriptures referring to himself.

They arrived at the town where they were going, and he kept walking as though he would continue on through. They warmly invited him in, saying, "Please stay with us, because it's late and the day is already over." So he went in to stay with them.

At supper time he took the bread and blessed it. Then he broke it and passed it to them. At that it dawned on them, and they recognized him!

And he became invisible.

They said to one another, "Weren't our hearts on fire inside of us while he was talking to us along the way and explaining the Scriptures to us?"

So they got right up, late as it was, and went back to Atlanta. There they found the eleven and some others gathered with them

---

[15]Literally, this passage means "to enter into his glory," i.e., to be inaugurated as rightful ruler, with all the attendant pomp and power.

who were saying, "The Master has really and truly risen! Simon saw him!"

Then *they* began rehearsing all that had occurred along the road, and how they had recognized him when he broke the bread.

36. Even as they were discussing these things, Jesus himself stood in their midst. They were scared out of their wits and almost took off, because they thought they were seeing a ghost.

He said, "Why are you shaking so? And why are your minds so filled with doubts? Take a look at my hands. And my feet. See, it's me. Feel me. And keep looking. A *ghost* doesn't have flesh and bones, as you can clearly see that I have."

And while they were busting out all over with joy, and wondering if they could believe their own eyes, he asked, "Have you got anything around here to eat?"

Somebody brought him a piece of fried fish. He took it and ate it right there in front of them.

He said to them, "All this is what I was talking about while I was still with you—how everything written about me in the law of Moses and in the Prophets and Psalms, had to take place."

Then he gave them the insight to understand the Scriptures.

44. And he said to them, "The Scriptures said that the Leader would suffer and be raised from the dead on the third day, and that there would be proclaimed in his name a change of attitude based on the giving up of sins against all races. Beginning in Atlanta, you all are the ones who'll make these things real. And listen, I myself am calling forth my Father's blessing on you. You all just stay right here in the city until you are charged with power from above."

50. He led them out toward College Park, and put his arms around them and blessed them. As he blessed them, he withdrew from them.

They went back into Atlanta with bounding joy. And they were continually in the church, praising God.

Happenings
[ACTS]

Happenings [ACTS]

1.

1. I wrote the first volume, Friend of God, about the many deeds and lessons which Jesus got under way, up to the day when he ascended. Prior to this he had given, through the Holy Spirit, specific orders to his special agents, and had shown himself to them with many positive proofs that he was still alive even after he had been killed. Through forty days he appeared to them and discussed matters concerning the God Movement. And while staying with them, he urged them not to leave Atlanta but to wait for the Father's promised gift about which he had told them. "Yes, John dipped people in water," he said, "but in just a few days you all will be dipped in Holy Spirit."

6. So those about him began asking, "Will that be the occasion on which you will take over the government?" He said to them, "You are not to get all worked up about timetables and events which the Father has under his own control. But as the Holy Spirit comes over you, you will get power and will be my agents in Atlanta and throughout Georgia, in the ghetto and across the land." As he said this, and while they were watching, he was carried away and a cloud kept them from seeing him.

10. As he went away, and while they were still staring into the sky, two men in blue jeans joined them and asked, "Citizens of America, why stand there looking at the sky? This Jesus who was carried away from you into the sky will come just as you saw him going into the sky."

12. Then they returned to Atlanta from "Peach Hill Orchard," which is in the suburbs of Atlanta. When they got back, they went upstairs where they were living. This included Rock and Jack and Jim and Andy, Phil and Tom, Bart and Matt, Jim Alston and Simon the Rebel, and Joe Jameson. All of them, including the women and Mary, Jesus' mother, and his brothers, were continually praying together.

15. While this was going on, Rock arose and said to the brotherhood (the number in the assembly was about one hundred twenty): "Brothers, it was inevitable that David's inspired prediction about Judas being in cahoots with those who framed Jesus, should come true. He belonged to our group, and thereby obtained a rightful share in this undertaking."

(It was he, you know, who with his bribe money bought a plot, where he fell and busted open, and his guts spilled out. That's why the people around Atlanta refer to it as "The Blood Plot.")

20. Rock continued, "In the book of Psalms it says,

> 'May his barn be empty
> and his house be vacant;'

also,

> 'Let someone else take over his office.'

"So, we've got to choose someone to join with us as evidence of Jesus' aliveness—someone who has been with us throughout the whole time Jesus was among us—from the beginning at John's baptism until the day of his ascension."

23. They then nominated two, George Jones, who was nicknamed Barsey, and Matt. They prayed and said, "You, Lord, heartknower of all, please make clear which one of these two you have selected to receive the rightful share of this undertaking and commission from which Judas deserted to go his own way." They had them draw lots, and the share fell to Matt, who was then counted in with the eleven officers.

2.

1. When Thanksgiving Day arrived, they were all gathered in one place. Then all of a sudden there came from the sky a rumbling like a tornado, and it filled the whole house where they were gathered. And they saw forked flames as from a fire, and it stayed in contact with each one of them. Everybody was bursting with Holy Spirit and started talking in whatever different languages the spirit directed.

5. Now at that time there were a lot of delegates gathered in Atlanta, religious people from countries all over the world. So when they heard this great noise, they all came running together. And then they heard these folks talking to each one of them in their own native tongue, and were they excited! Amazed and astounded no end, they said, "Look, aren't all these speakers Americans? Then how is it that each of us is hearing it in his own native tongue—French, Spanish, German, Portuguese, Chinese, Russian, Italian, Greek, Turkish, Burmese, Hebrew, Swedish, Afrikaans, Hindi—in our *own* languages we are hearing them tell of God's mighty doings." Everybody was dumfounded and puzzled, saying one to another, "What's the meaning of this?" But others sneered, "They're tanked up on white lightning."

14. So Rock, along with the eleven, got right up and started explaining matters to them: "Fellow Georgians and all you delegates in Atlanta, let me set you straight on this right now. These folks are not tanked up like you think, because it's just nine o'clock in the morning. Instead, this is the happening described in the book of Joel:

'When the time is ripe,' says God,
'I will share my spirit with all mankind,
And your sons and your daughters will speak the truth.
Your young people will catch visions

And your old people will dream new dreams.
Yes indeed, when the time is ripe I'll share my spirit
With my boys and my girls and they will speak the truth.
And I will put terrors in the sky above
And nightmares on the earth below—
Blood and fire and a mushroom cloud.
The sun will be turned into blackness
And the moon into blood,
When the glory and the majesty of the Lord's Era
Will be ushered in.
And then, the man who shares in the Lord's nature will
    come through.'

"Brother men, give me your attention. Surely you yourselves
know about Jesus, the Valdostan, a man whom God backed up
with the mighty deeds, marvelous happenings and solid evidence
which he presented right before your eyes. Within the framework
of his purpose and knowledge, God let you murder him by stringing him up at the hands of a mob. But then God removed the
effects of death and restored him to life. It just wasn't possible for
him to be contained by death. David puts these words on his lips:

'I was assured in advance of my Lord's abiding presence;
He is right beside me to keep me from being knocked out.
That's why my heart sings out and my tongue shouts for
    joy.
And even more, my whole body will be vibrant with
    hope;
Because you will not abandon my life to the grave,
Nor give your "divine spark" to the despair of death.
You have let me in on life's secrets;
With your presence you will make me unspeakably
    happy.'

"Brothers of mine, let me tell you bluntly that our forefather

David died, was buried and his tomb is still with us. But since he was a prophet, and knowing that God had guaranteed that one of his own descendants would succeed him, he foresaw the resurrection of the Leader when he referred to him as not being abandoned to the grave, nor his body to the despair of death. And it's this man Jesus that God has made alive, and all of us are the evidence of his aliveness. Since he has been elevated as 'God's right hand man,' and having received from the Father the assurance of the Holy Spirit, he has shared with us this which you are seeing and hearing. For while David himself never entered the spiritual realm, he did say,

"The Boss said to my boss, 'Be my right hand man while I put even your opponents under your control.' " Therefore let all America know beyond any doubt that God has made this same Jesus, whom you lynched, both President and Leader."

37. Upon hearing this they were cut to the quick, and they said to Rock and the other officers, "Will you please tell us, brothers, what we can do about it?"

Rock said to them, "Reshape your lives, and let each of you be initiated into the family of Jesus Christ so your sins can be dealt with; and you will receive the free gift of the Holy Spirit. For the guarantee is to you and your relatives, as well as to all the outsiders whom the Lord our God shall invite." Rock was going down the line on other matters, too, and kept urging them on. "Save yourselves," he was telling them, "from this goofed-up society."

41. So those who accepted his explanation were initiated, swelling the membership to about three thousand. They were all bound together by the officers' instruction and by the sense of community, by the common meal and the prayers. A great reverence came over everybody, while many amazing and instructive things were done by the officers. The whole company of believers stuck together and held all things common. They were selling

95

their goods and belongings, and dividing them among the group on the basis of one's need. Knit together with singleness of purpose they gathered at the church every day, and as they ate the common meal from house to house they had a joyful and humble spirit, praising God and showing over-flowing kindness toward everybody. And day by day, as people were being rescued, the Lord would add them to the fellowship.

3.

1. Now one afternoon about three o'clock, Rock and Jack were going into the church to pray. So there was this guy who was born a cripple and who was put every day at the main entrance of the sanctuary, to panhandle from those going to church. When he saw Rock and Jack about to go in, he started putting the bite on them. So Rock, with Jack backing him up, looked the fellow in the eye and said, "Look straight at us!" He smiled big at them, thinking they were a soft touch. Then Rock said, "I don't have one thin dime, but I'm going to give you what I do have. In the name of Jesus Christ of Valdosta, WALK!" And grabbing him by the right hand, Rock pulled him to his feet. Instantly he got strength in his feet and ankles and started jumping around and walking all over. He went with them into the church, walking and jumping and shouting God's praises. Everybody recognized him as the panhandler at the main entrance to the church and they were utterly amazed and astounded at what had happened to him.

11. While he was still hanging on to Rock and Jack, the whole congregation gathered around them in the vestibule. When Rock saw what was happening, he said to them all, "My fellow church members, why are you so surprised at this, or why are you staring at us as though this man has been made to walk by our own power or saintliness? The God of Abraham, Isaac and Jacob, the God of our fathers, has exalted this man Jesus, whom you all framed and disowned before the governor, and decided that he should be killed. But you disowned the Special One, the Just One, and asked that a convicted murderer be made your leader. While indeed you assassinated life's noblest one, God raised him from the dead, of which fact we all are the evidence. And his name—by faith in his name—this man whom you see and recognize has received strength. The faith that came through Jesus made him normal before your eyes.

17. "And now, brothers, I am aware that you did it without realizing what you were up to, and the same is true of your leaders. In fact, in this way God has made a reality of what he previously announced through the sermons of all the prophets, about his Leader choosing to suffer. Re-shape your lives, then, and turn around, so that the slate can be wiped clean of your past misdeeds, that opportunities for renewal might come to you from the Lord, and that he might send to you Jesus, his previously chosen Leader. It's necessary for this leader to remain in the spiritual realm only until the occasions leading up to the establishment of everything God said long ago, through his genuine prophets. Indeed, Moses himself said, 'The Lord your God will provide for you from among your own kinsmen a prophet like me. You shall follow the instructions *he* gives you to the very last detail. If there's a soul who won't listen to *that* prophet, he shall be utterly rooted out of the congregation.' Furthermore, from Samuel on down, all the prophets discussed and described what's happening right now. You folks are in this stream of prophecy and are heirs of the contract which God drew up with your forefathers when he said to Abraham, 'And through your descendant all the nations on earth shall be given a new lease on life.' Now that God has just raised up his man, you are first in line to receive the new lease when each of you turns from his mean ways."

4.

1. They were still talking to the people when some preachers and the police chief and the Old Guard laid into them. They were plenty mad at them because they were teaching the people and declaring that Jesus was raised from the dead. So they had them arrested and put in jail until the next day, since it was already late in the evening. Many of those who heard the word were convinced, and the number of men rose to about five thousand.

5. Well, the next day the leading men and the city officials and the legal staff met in Atlanta. (These included Anderson, the mayor, and Cates and John and Alec, and others on the City Council.) They had Rock and Jack stand up front, and they began the hearing by asking, "By what authority or in whose name have you fellows done this?" Then Rock, busting with Holy Spirit, said to them, "Leaders of the people and city officials, if we today are being examined because of a good work done on a sick man, that is—who has healed him—let it be made clear to you and to everybody in America, that in the name of Jesus of Valdosta, whom you lynched, whom God made to live again, by him this man stands before you completely healed. Indeed, this Jesus is 'the stone which you builders considered worthless, but which became the corner stone.' And the answer lies in him alone, for there isn't another person in the whole world who can rescue us."

13. The officials were really surprised at the boldness of Rock and Jack, especially since they seemed to be uneducated and simple people, and it dawned on them that these were Jesus' pupils. On top of this, they saw the healed man standing there with them, and couldn't argue that point. So they told them to step outside the courtroom, and then they started discussing the matter. "What'll we do with these fellows? For it's as clear as day to everybody in Atlanta that they've done something terrific, and we simply can't deny it. But, to keep this from blowing all over the country, let's read the riot act to them, that they are never again to mention this man's name to a living soul."

18. So they called them back in and started throwing the book at them, warning them never to open their mouths on the subject of Jesus. But Rock and Jack spoke right up and said, "You can make up your own minds as to whether it's right to obey God or man. But as for us, it's impossible to keep quiet about what we've seen and heard."

21. When the officials had finished putting the heat on them, they ran them off. They could find no way to punish them, because of their standing with the crowd. Everybody was praising God for what had happened, since the man who had been so wonderfully healed was over forty years old.

23. After they were turned loose, they went straight to the fellowship and rehearsed all that the officials had said to them. Upon hearing it, all of them lifted up a united voice to God and said, "Mighty Owner, Maker of land and sky and sea and all that's in them, through the Holy Spirit you moved your servant and our father David to say,

'Why have the pagans pranced around,
And the crowds put on such airs?
The power structure of the nation lined up together,
And the important people took their stand
Against the Lord and His appointed Leader.'

Surely in this very city both the Governor of Alabama and the Governor of Georgia have gotten together with church members and non-church members against your devoted servant Jesus, whom you authorized to carry out the things you wanted done. And now, Sir, listen to their threats and give us, your slaves, the guts to tell your word like it is, while you reach out to heal and to do great and wonderful things by the name of your devoted servant Jesus." When they finished praying, the place where they were meeting was shaken. And they were all filled with the Holy Spirit, and were telling God's word like it is.

32. Now a single heart and soul was in the body of believers. Not one of them considered his property to be private, but all things were shared by them. With mighty power the apostles were giving the evidence of Jesus' aliveness, and upon them all was a spirit of abounding goodwill. You know, there wasn't a person in the group in need. For owners of land or houses were selling them and bringing the proceeds and placing them at the disposal of the apostles. Distribution was then made to everyone on the basis of his need.

36. So, a fellow named Joe (his nickname, "Barney," given to him by the apostles, means "a helpful guy"), from an old-line Virginia family, owned a farm. He sold it, brought the proceeds and placed them at the disposal of the church officers.[1] *But*, there was a man by the name of Harry who sold a piece of property and held back some of the money. His wife, Sapphire, was also in on the deal. He then brought a certain part[2] and put it at the disposal of the officers. But Rock said to him, "Harry, why are you so full of the devil that you've lied to the Holy Spirit and kept some of the money from the sale of the land? Wasn't the property yours all along, and didn't you make the decision to sell it? Then what came over you to do a thing like this? You are not playing false with men but with God!"

5. While Harry was listening to what was being said, he collapsed and died. And it scared the daylights out of all those who

---

[1] I am omitting the Chapter 5 heading here, for it rudely interrupts the original narrative which contrasts the two differing responses to the fellowship's policy of sharing all things with one another.

[2] Possibly the part prescribed by the Jewish law—the tithe.

were watching. The ushers then got up, put a sheet over him, carried him outside and buried him.

7. Well, about three hours later, in walked his wife, without knowing what had gone on. Rock asked her, "Tell me, did you get such and such for the land? She said, "Yes, that's correct." Then Rock said to her, "Why did you two conspire to confuse the Lord's spirit? Listen here, the men who buried your husband are coming in the door and they'll take you out!" Right then and there she collapsed at his feet and died. The ushers came on in, and finding her dead, too, took her out and buried her beside her husband. The whole church and all who heard about it were evermore shook up!

12. The officers did a lot of other remarkable and wonderful things among the people. They were meeting together at Grant Park, and while nobody was brave enough to join them, folks did speak mighty highly of them. But increasingly quite a group of both men and women put their faith in the Lord and were enrolled. Besides, the sick were carried into the streets and put on cots and stretchers so that even Rock's shadow might fall on them as he passed by. Also, crowds from the towns all around Atlanta flocked in, bringing those sick in body and mind, and they were all healed.

17. But the Mayor and City Council, who were members of the Conservative Party, blew their top. They arrested the apostles and put them in the city jail. But that night, an angel of the Lord opened the jailhouse doors, led them outside and said, "Go, stand on the courthouse steps and explain to the people all the matters concerning this kind of life." They listened carefully, and at the crack of day they went to the courthouse steps and started teaching. Now the mayor and his assistants called a meeting of the Council and all the prominent white citizens, and sent to fetch the apostles. But when the fuzzes got to the clink, they didn't find the apostles in it. They went back and reported: "We found the jail-house locked according to regulations and the guards were on duty, but when we opened up and went inside we didn't find a soul." When the police chief and the Council heard this, they tried to figure out what the hell had happened. About that time somebody came busting in and shouted, "Hey, those joes you put in the jug are standing on the courthouse steps preaching to the people." Then the chief and his fuzzes went out and got them without using brutality, because they were scared the crowd might throw bottles at them. They led them in and stood them up before the Council. The mayor tore into them and said, "We warned you in no uncertain terms not to spread the ideas of that fellow. And now look, you've agitated all of Atlanta with your ideas, and are trying to pin that guy's lynching on us!"

29. Rock and the other officers replied, "It's our duty to obey God rather than men. Our fathers' God raised Jesus, whom you mobbed and strung up on a tree. God promoted *him* to be his number one Leader and Deliverer, to bring to white folks a change of heart and a way out of their sins. And all of us are evidence of this statement, as indeed is the Holy Spirit which God gives to those who are controlled by him."

33. At this the city fathers blew a gasket and wanted to kill them on the spot. But a Baptist by the name of Gamaliel, a Sunday School teacher with a good reputation in the community, got up in the Council and ordered the apostles to be put outside for a little while. Then he said, "My fellow citizens, be extremely careful in your actions against these men. A while back, you remember, Turner set himself up as a big-time movement man and got about four hundred people to join up. But he was rubbed out, his followers routed, and they got nowhere. Later on, when the draft law was passed, Jody the Tennessean made a stir and got quite a following, but he too was wiped out and his movement broken up. So, in this situation I'd advise you to keep your hands off these men

102

and let them be. If this plan or this program of theirs is a purely human scheme, it will blow itself out. But if it is God's thing, you can't put a stop to it without declaring yourselves at war with God." That made sense to them, so they called in the apostles, beat them up, warned them not to talk about Jesus anymore, and turned them loose. The apostles then left the Council meeting, happy that they were counted worthy to be disgraced for the Name. Every day, both on the courthouse steps and from door to door, they never quit teaching and preaching that Jesus is Lord.

6.

1. Along about the time that a lot of members were coming into the church, the liberals got into a hassle with the conservatives because some of their dependents were being discriminated against in the distribution of relief funds. So the twelve called a meeting of the whole church and said, "It's not a good idea for us to take time away from the teaching of God's word to tend to material matters. So brothers, why don't you choose seven reliable men who are spiritual-minded and wise, and we'll commission them to take this responsibility? Then we can give full time to prayer and to the cultivation of the word." This suggestion pleased the congregation, so they nominated Steve, a deeply spiritual fellow who was on fire for the faith, and Phil and Proctor and Nick and Timmie and Farmer and Nichol, a former church member from up North. These were recommended to the officers, who then prayed for them and commissioned them.

7. The word of God made much headway. The number of converts in Atlanta increased tremendously, with a goodly portion even of the ministerial association becoming Christians.

8. Now Steve, loaded with good will and energy, was doing all sorts of terrific things among the people. Then some cats from the so-called conservative church—from Kentucky and Tennessee and some from the True-God Seminary and Bible College—ganged up on Steve and started arguing with him, but they couldn't hold a candle to his wise and inspired answers. They got their cronies to say, "We heard him saying some awful things against God and the Bible." They stirred up the good citizens and the official power structure, and grabbed Steve and arrested him and brought him before the Council. They brought in some professional liars who said, "This joker never stops blabbing against the church and against the system. For we ourselves heard him say that this Jesus of Valdosta will destroy the church and will change the American way of life." All those sitting in the Council glued their eyes on him. They noticed he had a look on him like an angel.

7.

1. Then the Mayor asked, "Are these things true?" And Steve said, "My fellow Americans and gentlemen, please listen to me.[3] The Good Lord appeared to our forefather Abraham while he was still in Mesopotamia, and before he moved to Haran, and said to him, 'Leave your native land and your relatives, and come into a land that I will show you.' Then he left Chaldea and went to Haran. After his father died, he migrated to this country in which you now live. But God gave him no homestead in it—not even an acre. Yet he did guarantee that it would belong to him and to his line, though at that time he was childless. Here's how God put it:

'His line will be pilgrims in a strange land, and they will be exploited and mistreated for four hundred years. And I will judge the nation which exploits them.' God said, 'and afterwards they will move out and worship me in this country.' And he gave to him circumcision as the symbol of the new life. Being thus initi-

---

[3]Because there is no modern parallel to the historical situation here described by Stephen, we return to the original setting.

ated, he became the father of Isaac, whom he initiated on the eighth day. And Isaac did the same to his son Jacob, and Jacob to his sons, the twelve founding fathers.

9. "Now the founding fathers were jealous of Joseph and sold him into Egypt. But God was with him and pulled him through all his trials, and supplied him with tact and common sense when he stood before Pharaoh, King of Egypt. So the King appointed him to be governor over Egypt and all his affairs. Now a famine which caused great hardship came over the whole of Egypt and Canaan, and our fathers could find no rations. But Jacob caught wind of some wheat in Egypt and sent his boys down there for the first time. On the second trip, Joseph let his brothers know who he was, and he also informed Pharaoh about his family. Then Joseph sent and fetched the whole shebang—his father Jacob and about seventy-five relatives. So Jacob moved to Egypt, and he and our founding fathers lived there till they died. They were later moved and put in a burial place in Sechem which Abraham had bought for cash from a Sechem family named Herman.

17. "As the time approached for God to make good on the guarantee he had made to Abraham, our population in Egypt had greatly increased and there was a king over Egypt who had forgotten all about Joseph. He didn't shoot straight with our people and was so mean he made the fathers abandon their babies to die. During this period, Moses, a very special child, was born. He was cared for at home for three months, and when he was "abandoned," Pharaoh's daughter adopted him and raised him as her own son. Moses was given a top-notch Egyptian education, and was a powerful man in both what he said and did.

23. "When he was about forty, it was laid on his heart to investigate the conditions of his own Jewish people. While doing so, he saw one of them getting beat up, and he jumped in and squared things away for the Israelite by knocking hell out of the Egyptian. He took for granted that his brothers would get the point that

God would use him to be their Freedom Leader. But they didn't catch on. In fact, the very next day he chanced on two of them slugging one another, and he tried to get them to break it up. 'Hey you guys,' he said, 'you're brothers. How come you beating up on each other?' But the fellow who started the fight shoved Moses aside and said, 'Who put you in the big seat to lord it over us? Do you think you can bump me off just like you bumped off that Egyptian yesterday?' When Moses heard that, he high-tailed it out of there and became a resident of Midian. His two boys were born there.

30. "Forty years later he was in the open country around Mt. Sinai when an angel appeared to him in the flames of a bush that was on fire. When Moses saw it he couldn't believe his eyes. So he went over to investigate, and then the Lord started speaking. 'I am the God of your forefathers—Abraham and Isaac and Jacob.' That got Moses shook up and he was scared to do any more investigating. But the Lord continued, 'Take off your shoes, because you're standing on holy ground. I have seen the awful oppression of my people in Egypt; I have listened to their moanings; I stand ready now to free them. So come on, I'm sending you to Egypt.'

35. "This very same Moses, whom they rejected by saying, 'Who put you in the big seat to lord it over us,' was sent by God through the angel at the Bush, to be both Leader and Liberator. This Moses worked amazing but clear proofs in Egypt and at the Red Sea, and led the people out into open country and guided them for forty years. This is the Moses who stood between the angel, speaking from Mt. Sinai, and our fathers gathered in the open country; who received the Living Words and relayed them to us. Yes, he is the one whom our fathers were unwilling to obey and shoved aside. They lapsed into the Egypt mentality, and said to Aaron, 'Make us some gods who will stick by us, because "this Moses," who led us out of Egypt, we just don't know what he's up to.'

41. "So they made a calf during those days, and celebrated with a big feast to the idol, and they whooped it up around their own invention. But God walked out and left them to worship the whole galaxy of gods, just as it is written in the book of the prophets: 'Was it to *me*, O nation of Israel, that you made your celebrations and feasts those forty years in the open country? No indeed, but you made War your god, and Violence your guiding star. They became patterns of your worship. All right, I'll banish you to outer Babylon.'

44. "While in the open country our fathers had a Chapel of the Presence, built according to the plan which God described to Moses. In the next generation, under Joshua, it was moved into the Promised Land which God cleared of pagans to make room for our people, and there it stayed until the time of David. Now David got the idea of putting up a more plush sanctuary for the God of Jacob, but Solomon actually built it. *But—*

THE ALMIGHTY DOES NOT LIVE IN MAN-MADE BUILDINGS.

The prophet bears this out when he says,

> 'The sky is my office,
> The earth is my den, says the Lord,
> 'What kind of a house could *you* build *me*,
> Or what kind of a resting place,
> Seeing as how I've made everything already?'

51. "You pig-headed pagans, you are forever turning a deaf ear to the Holy Spirit. You are just like your fathers before you. Can you name just one man of God that they didn't ride out on a rail? And besides, they assassinated the forerunners of the Just One. And now *you* are *his* betrayers and killers—you who got the Bible straight from angels, and refused to live by it!"

54. When they heard this they were cut to the quick, and hit the ceiling. Steve, however, vibrant with the Holy Spirit, fastened

107

his eyes on the sky and saw God's glory, and Jesus standing as God's right-hand man. He cried out, "Look, I'm seeing the skies opening up and the Son of Man is standing beside God as his right-hand man." But they yelled bloody murder and put their fingers in their ears. Then all together they gave him the bum's rush, dragged him out of town and started throwing rocks at him. Those taking part in it piled their coats in front of a young fellow named Saul. They kept on throwing rocks at Steve while he was calling on Jesus, saying, "Lord Jesus, please accept my soul." Then he knelt down and cried out with all he had, "O Lord, don't charge them with this crime." Having said this, he fell asleep. Now Saul was justifying the murder.

8.

1. At that time a great persecution broke out against the Atlanta fellowship, and all except the officers were scattered through the white and black sections of Georgia. Some deeply concerned men gathered Steve up and gave him a decent funeral. But Saul was putting the heat on the church, searching through house after house and dragging out both men and women and throwing them in jail.

4. As they were scattered, though, they spread the good news of the faith all over. Phil, for example, went over to a city of black people and was telling them all about the Leader. As the crowds listened to Phil and watched the terrific things he was doing, they hung on to every word he was saying. Quite a few of them who had mean spirits gave them up with loud sobs. Others who were disabled and crippled were healed. A spirit of joyful hope swept over the whole community.

9. Now for some time a rabble-rouser named Simpson had lived in that town and, by posing as a big-time leader, he had bamboozled the black people. Old and young alike trekked after him. "He's got the guts of God, man," they said. "He's talking Power." He had fed them with his poppycock so long that they actually believed it. But when they accepted Phil's explanation of the God Movement and what it meant to be a Christian, both men and women were being baptized. Even Simpson himself became a convert, and after his baptism he hung around Phil so he could keep a close eye on how he worked miracles and did fabulous things.

14. Well, the apostles in Atlanta heard that "Harlem" had come over to the Word of God, so they sent Rock and Jack there. When they arrived, they prayed for them that they might receive Holy Spirit. For as yet they had only been baptized into the church and Holy Spirit had not possessed any of them. Then the apostles laid their hands on them and they received Holy Spirit.

18. Simpson noticed that the Spirit came with the laying on of the officers' hands, so he propositioned them with a wad of money. "Let me in on the deal," he said, "so that whenever I put my hands on somebody he'll get Holy Spirit."

Rock said to him, "You and your money can go to hell! Do you think you can *buy* with money what God freely *gives?* You have no part or parcel in this faith, because your soul isn't straight in God's sight. Quit this mean thing of yours, and beg the Lord to forgive the perversion of your soul, for I can tell that you are enslaved to bitterness and imprisoned by crookedness."

"You all beg the Lord for me," Simpson cried, "that what you said about me might not come true."

25. After Rock and Jack had told the Word of God like it is, and had preached it all around, they went back to Atlanta, explaining the Good News to blacks they met along the way.

26. Now a messenger of the Lord said to Phil, "Get ready and go south along the road that goes from Atlanta to LaGrange."

(It's open country through there.) So he got ready and went. At the same time there was a high-up official of Tuskegee—the treasurer, in fact—who had gone to a convention in Atlanta. He was going home and sitting on the bus reading from Isaiah. So the spirit said to Phil, "Flag that bus!" So he flagged it and got on and saw the man reading from Isaiah. Phil asked him, "Does what you're reading make sense?" The man replied "How can I make heads or tails of it when there's no one to explain it to me?" Then he asked Phil to sit beside him. The passage he was reading was this:

"He was led off to slaughter like a sheep;
As a lamb which makes no sound when it is clipped,
So he uttered no word of protest.
In his humiliation, justice was denied him.
As for his children, who will remember them?
His earthly lineage will be no more."

34. The treasurer said to Phil, "Let me ask you a question. To whom is the prophet referring here, to himself or to someone else?" Then Phil began with this passage and explained Jesus to him. Along the way they came to a stream, and the treasurer said, "Look, there's a stream! Why can't I be baptized now?" So he told the bus driver to stop, and both Phil and the treasurer got off and went down to the stream, where Phil baptized him. When they came up out of the stream, the spirit of the Lord grabbed Phil, and the treasurer never saw him again, but he headed off toward Tuskegee singing happily. However, Phil was located in Anniston, and as he traveled he was spreading the good word through all the towns as far as Huntsville.

9.

1. All the while, Saul was harassing and threatening to kill the followers of the Lord. He even went to the governor and got some papers to the Chattanooga Council asking them for permission to arrest and return to Atlanta any men or women he might find who were taking Christianity seriously. When he stopped for gas just outside of Chattanooga, all of a sudden a flash from the sky surrounded him. He fell to the pavement, and heard a voice asking, "Saul! Saul! Why are you so mean to me?"

He said, "Who are you, sir?"

"I," he said, "I am Jesus whom you're harassing . . . But get up now and go on into the city and it will be made clear to you what you've got to do."

The fellows traveling with him just stood there speechless. They heard the sound but saw nobody. Saul got up from the pavement, but when he opened his eyes he couldn't see a thing. They led him to the car and took him on into Chattanooga. For three days he was blind, and he ate nothing and drank nothing.

10. In Chattanooga there was a Christian named Harry. He had a vision and heard the Lord calling his name. "Harry!" And Harry said, "I'm right here, sir." Then the Lord said to him, "Get ready and go over to Joe's house on Straight Street and ask for a fellow by the name of Saul, who comes from Tallahassee. He is praying right now, and has had a vision of a person named Harry coming in and putting his hands on him so he may see again."

Harry replied, "Sir, I have learned from many people all the terrible things which this fellow has done to your followers in Atlanta. He has even come here with warrants from the officials to arrest all who hear your name."

But the Lord said to him, "Get moving, for this man is a very special instrument which I have chosen to represent me before the people of the world and their leaders, as well as the 'good white people'. For I myself will make clear to him all he must go through to bear my name."

17. So Harry left and went to the house. He put his hands on Saul and said, "Saul . . . brother . . . the Lord . . . er . . . Jesus whom

you saw on the way here . . . has sent me . . . that you may be able
to see and that you may be filled with Holy Spirit." And right away
something like scales fell from his eyes and he could see. He got
ready and was baptized. Then he ate something, felt stronger, and
decided to stay on with the converts in Chattanooga for some time.

20. Soon he began preaching in their churches that Jesus truly
is God's man.[4] All that heard him were simply bowled over, and
said, "Why, ain't this the guy that gave hell to those in Atlanta
who bear the Name? And hasn't he come up here for the sole
purpose of arresting them and taking them back to the officials?"
But Saul took an even stronger stand and out-argued the white
American Protestants (WAPs) in Chattanooga, proving beyond
doubt that Jesus is indeed Lord.[5]

23. After some days had passed, the WAPs hatched a plot to
kill him. Saul, however, got wind of their plot. Day and night they
spied on his hotel, hoping for a chance to assassinate him. But the
brothers lowered him one night from a back window into an alley.
He took off for Atlanta, and tried to join up with the converts
there. But they were all scared of him, because they couldn't believe that he was a genuine convert. However, Barney took up for
him and introduced him to the officers. He explained to them how
Saul, on his trip, had seen the Lord, who had spoken to him, and
how that in Chattanooga he made no bones about being a disciple
of Jesus. So he stayed with them, operating in and out of Atlanta,
fearlessly bearing the name of the Lord, and getting into discussions and debates with the Klan. They figured they would liquidate
him, so when the apostles found out about it, they took him to
Griffin and put him on the bus to Tallahassee.

31. Then the brotherhood throughout Georgia, Alabama and

---

[4]Or, Son, i.e., the titular head of the God Movement. Jesus' own favorite
designation of himself was "son of man."

[5]Or, Christ. It is equivalent to "Son" in vs. 20, and again refers to Jesus
as God's designated Leader of the God Movement.

Tennessee had peace. It was built up, and with reverence for the Lord and encouraged by the Holy Spirit, it stayed on course and grew.

32. It so happened that on one of Rock's many trips he stopped off with the converts living at Waycross. He found a man there named Ames who was paralyzed and had been bedfast for eight years. And Rock said to him, "Mr. Ames, Jesus Christ is healing you. Get up and put on your clothes." And did he get up! A lot of people in Waycross and around Blackshear saw the man and came over to the Lord's side.

36. In Brunswick there was a lady believer named Dorcas (her name means "a deer"). She was noted for her many kind and charitable acts. One day she got sick and died. After they had bathed her they put her in the upstairs parlor. Since Waycross is fairly close to Brunswick, and the disciples had heard that Rock was over there, they sent two men with this urgent message: "Please don't waste a second getting over here." So he quick got ready and went with them. When he arrived he went into the upstairs parlor where a lot of widows had gathered, and they were sobbing as they showed him the coats and dresses Dorcas had made for them while she was alive. Rock asked them all to please leave the room, and he knelt down and prayed. He then turned his attention to the body. "Dorcas," he said, "get up!" She opened her eyes, looked at Rock, and sat up. He gave her his hand and helped her to her feet. Then he called in the believers and the widows and presented her to them—alive! This spread throughout Brunswick, and many put their faith in the Lord. Rock stayed quite a while in Brunswick at the home of a barber named Smith.

10.

1. Now there was a man in Augusta by the name of Cornwall, a Negro captain stationed at Ft. Gordon. He was a spiritually sensitive person, and with his whole family he sought God's will. He did a lot of volunteer work for the poor and he lived prayerfully. One day about three in the afternoon he had an extremely clear vision of a messenger from God entering and saying to him, "Cornwall!" Scared to death, he looked the messenger in the face and asked, "What is it, sir?" The messenger replied, "God has been noticing your prayerfulness and your unselfish deeds. Now you must send some men to Brunswick to pick up a fellow named Simon, or Rock, as he is nicknamed. He is staying with Smith, the barber, whose house faces the sea."

7. After the messenger finished and left, Cornwall called two trusted friends and an understanding soldier who was in his prayer group, and related his experience to them. He then asked that they go to Brunswick.

9. The next day, while they were traveling toward the city, Rock went upstairs about noon to pray. He got so hungry he could hardly wait to eat. While the folks were fixing lunch, Rock fell into a trance, and he saw a hole in the sky and an outfit like a big four-cornered tablecloth being let down to the ground. In it were all kinds of meat, seafood and fowl. About that time he heard somebody call, "Come on, Rock, sit down and let's eat!" But Rock said, "Oh no, sir, I've never eaten anything that was inferior or not kosher." The voice said once, and then repeated, "If God makes something kosher, don't you treat it as dirty." This was said a third time, and then the whole outfit was pulled back up into the sky.

17. While Rock was trying to figure out what his vision was all about, the fellows who had been sent by Cornwall had gotten directions to Smith's house and were ringing the doorbell. When someone answered, the men inquired if Simon, who was called Rock, was staying there. As Rock still pondered on his vision, the Spirit said to him, "Listen, two men are looking for you! Get up, go downstairs and go with them without the slightest hesitation, for I have sent them." So Rock went downstairs and said to the man, "Look, I'm the fellow you want. Why have you come here?"

"Captain Cornwall, a good and devout man, as all white people will tell you," they said, "was instructed by God's messenger to invite you to his home and listen to what you have to tell him." So Rock asked them in and gave them hospitality.

23. The next day he packed up and went with them, taking several brothers from Brunswick with him. When they got to Augusta, Cornwall was waiting for them and had invited in a number of his kinfolks and close friends. As Rock came in, Cornwall greeted him, warmly shook his hand, and called him "mister." Rock corrected him, "Don't 'mister' me, for I am a human being the same as you." Well, they struck up a conversation and went on in, where the friends had gathered. Rock started talking to them. "Y'all understand how uncustomary it is for a white man to socialize or stay with people of a different race, don't you? All right, but as for me, God has made it plain as day to me that I'm never to think of any man as inferior or no good. That's why I came without batting an eye when I was sent for. Now may I ask what was in your mind when you sent for me?"

30. Cornwall spoke up, "Exactly four days ago to the hour, I was at home praying, around three p.m., when suddenly a man in clean new blue jeans appeared and said, 'Cornwall, God has been noticing your prayerfulness and your unselfish deeds. Now you must send to Brunswick and pick up Simon, whose nickname is Rock. He is staying at the home of Smith, the barber, on the sea coast.' So right away I sent for you, and you have honored us by coming. Now we are all gathered here before God to listen to whatever he has laid on your heart."

"I am convinced beyond any doubt," Rock began, "that God pays no attention to a man's skin. Regardless of his race, the man who respects God and practices justice is welcomed by him. This point was made clear to the white people when the good news of peace through Jesus Christ was preached. He indeed is Lord of *all* people. You all are getting to know the message which spread all over Georgia from its beginning in Alabama with John's baptism—the message about Jesus from Valdosta, how God equipped him with Holy Spirit and power, who passed through our midst acting nobly and helping all those who were lorded over by the devil, because God stood by him. We ourselves can testify to all that he did in the land of the whites right here in Atlanta, and how they lynched him, stringing him up on a tree. Three days later God raised him and let him be seen, not by the general public, but by witnesses which God had previously hand-picked—by us—who ate and drank with him after he was raised from the dead. And he commissioned us to carry the word and be the evidence that this Jesus has been established by God as the criterion for both the living and the dead. The whole Bible points to him—that everyone who bets his life on him receives forgiveness for his sins, for Jesus' sake."

44. Even as Rock was saying these words, Holy Spirit came over all the listeners. Even the white believers, who had accompanied Rock, were taken by surprise that the Holy Spirit was so freely given to other races. For they themselves were hearing them talking the language and shouting the praises of God. Then Rock asked, "Is anyone opposed to baptizing these people who have received Holy Spirit the same as we have?" So he ruled that they should be baptized into the Christian fellowship. Then they asked him to stay on with them as long as he could.

11.

1. Now the news spread to both preachers and laymen throughout Georgia that other races were responding to the word of God. So when Rock returned to Atlanta, some who believe in segregation, tore into him. "You went home with folks who aren't white," they shouted, "and you were *eating* with them!" Rock then got going and laid the matter out for them just like it happened:

"I was down there in Brunswick engaged in a bit of meditation, and in my ecstasy I had a vision. I saw this outfit coming down that looked like a big tablecloth being lowered by its four corners, and it came to where I was. When I looked inside of it I really got puzzled. For what did I see but meats of all kinds imaginable, and sea foods, and a complete assortment of fowl. Then I heard somebody calling me, 'Come on, Rock, sit down and eat.' But I said, 'Oh, no sir, I have never taken the first bite of anything that was inferior or wasn't strictly kosher.' Again the voice from the sky spoke: 'If God makes something kosher, don't you treat it as dirty.' This was repeated, and the whole business was pulled back up into the sky. And would you believe it, at that moment three men knocked on the door where I was staying. They had been sent there from Augusta. The Spirit told me to go with them without the slightest hesitation. I went, and took with me these six brothers. After we arrived at the guy's house he told us how he had seen the messenger standing in his house and saying, 'Send to Brunswick and fetch a Simon who goes by the nickname of Rock; he will give you some information on how you and your whole family may be rescued.'

"As I began to speak, the Holy Spirit came over them just as it had over us at the beginning. It reminded me of something the Lord had told us: 'John did dip people in water, but you all will be dipped in Holy Spirit.' Well, then, if God's gift to them was exactly the same as ours when we put our faith in the Lord Jesus Christ, what right did I have to argue with God?" Upon hearing this explanation, they came down off their high horse and started praising God. "Then it's a fact," they said, "that God has given to the Negroes the transformed life."

19. The people who had to leave because of the trouble which centered around Steve went as far as Florida, South Carolina and Mobile, spreading the word only among white folks. Some of them, though, from South Carolina and Kentucky, went to Mobile and were meeting with blacks, telling them the great news of the Lord Jesus. The Lord worked with them and a good number believed and went the Lord's Way.

22. Word reached the Atlanta church about them, and they sent Barney to Mobile. When he arrived and saw how God had favored them he was real pleased. He encouraged them all to put their whole heart in their commitment to the Lord, because he himself was a good guy, bursting with Holy Spirit and faithfulness. A big crowd was joining the Lord's Movement, so Barney checked out for Tallahassee to get Saul, and when he found him he brought him back to Mobile. They stayed there a whole year, meeting with the fellowship and teaching a sizeable crowd. And it was here in Mobile that the disciples were first labeled "Christians."

27. During the time that Barney and Saul were there, some preachers from Atlanta arrived in Mobile. One of them, by the name of Albert, made an inspired prediction that a terrible depression was going to hit the whole country, which actually happened when the Republicrats were in office. So it was decided by the disciples that each would give according to his means to the brothers who stayed on in Georgia. When they had collected the money, they sent it to the church officers by Barney and Saul.

12.

1. Along about then Governor Herod got a notion to do in some of those in the fellowship. He finished off Jim, Jack's brother, with a sword. Seeing that the "good white folks" were pleased at this, he decided to put the squeeze on Rock. (This happened during the week of Easter.) So he arrested him and put him in jail, and had him guarded by four shifts of officers with four in each shift. It was his intention to turn him over to the mob after Easter. And all the while that Rock was being kept in the clink, the fellowship was praying agonizingly for him.

6. Just before Herod was going to turn him over to the mob, Rock was sleeping that night between two guards. He was handcuffed to them, and the officers were on duty at the door. All of a sudden, a light shined in the cell and the Lord's messenger appeared. He hit Rock on his side, pulled him up, and said, "Get moving *fast*." His handcuffs. fell off. The messenger said to him, "Get dressed and put on your shoes." He did that. "Now put on your coat and let's go." He followed him outside, still not knowing that what the messenger was doing was for real, but thinking he was having a dream. They passed the first guard, then the second, and came to the big iron gate that opens on to the street. It opened automatically for them, and they walked out. They had gone about a block when all of a sudden the messenger left him.

11. When it finally dawned on Rock what had happened, he said, "Sure as I'm living the Lord sent his messenger and rescued me from Herod, and from all that that white mob expected to do."

12. He sized up the situation and went around to the house of Mary, Jack Mark's mother, where quite a crowd had gathered for prayer. He started banging on the door and a teen-ager named Rosie went to the door to answer it. When she recognized Rock's voice, instead of opening the door, she was so happy she ran back in and yelled that Rock was at the door. They said, "You're off your rocker." But she kept insisting that it was really and truly so. "Well, it must be his ghost," they said.

16. But Rock was still banging away at the door. They opened up and there he stood. And were they evermore surprised! He waved to them and told them to keep quiet while he described to

119

them how the Lord had got him out of the clink. "Now," he said, "y'all get word of all this to Jim and the brothers." Then he left and went somewhere else.

18. When day came there was one helluva hubbub among the guards over what had become of Rock. Herod looked high and low for him but couldn't find him. He got all the information he could from the guards, and ordered them to be shot. He then left Atlanta to visit a while in Augusta.

20. Now Governor Herod was having a knock-down, drag-out fight with the Education Commission and the Welfare Department. So they decided to get together and meet with him. They won over Blastus, the governor's chief aide, to see if he could settle the dispute, since all their funds came from the state's treasury. An appointment was made, and the governor showed up with great fanfare at the Capitol. He made a speech that was pure jazz, and all the big-wigs obediently praised him. "Inspired! God, not a mortal, made that speech!" Right then and there an angel of the Lord struck him down because he took God's credit. He had a heart attack and died.

24. But God's message continued to spread and win adherents. And Barney and Saul, when they had wound up things in Atlanta, returned and took with them John Mark.

13.

1. The preachers and teachers in the fellowship at Mobile consisted of Barney, Sumner Black, Lucius Cummings, Mansfield, a classmate of Governor Herod, and Saul. During a deeply meaningful worship service, the Holy Spirit directed, "Set apart Barney and Saul for some special work I have for them." Then they all fasted and prayed, after which they ordained them and sent them on their journey.

4. So then having been commissioned by the Holy Spirit, they went to Pensacola, and then caught a bus for Montgomery. They went on up to Birmingham and spread the word of God in the white churches there, taking John Mark along as general flunky. Next they went to Tuscaloosa, where they ran into a joker named "Reverend Jesus." He was a phony white preacher who was a friend of the mayor, Sergent Powell, a shrewd guy himself. The mayor sent for Barney and Saul and wanted to hear what the word of God was all about. However, Reverend Ellis (that was his real name) strenuously objected and did his best to sidetrack the mayor from the faith. Then Saul (or Paul as he was also called), running over with Holy Spirit, looked him in the eye and said, "You crooked creep! You low-down louse! You son of the devil! You full-time phony! You habitually twist God's clear message out of shape.⁶ All right, now listen, the Lord has put the finger on you and you'll be as blind as a bat for some time." Right then and there he was completely socked in and started wandering around looking for somebody to lead him by the hand. Then the mayor, seeing the way things had turned out—and shook up by the teaching of the Lord—began to live by the Unseen.

13. Then Paul and his party pulled out of Tuscaloosa and went to Meridian, Mississippi. There John Mark resigned and checked out for Atlanta. The others kept on going through Meridian till they came to Vicksburg. On a Sunday they went to a church and sat down. After the reading of the Scripture the minister said to them, "Brothers, if you have any helpful message for the congregation, we would be pleased to hear it."

16. Paul got up and went to the pulpit. "My fellow Baptists and all who are serious about God," he began, "please give me your attention. The God of us Southerners favored our forefathers

---

⁶The language in the original is sharp and brutal. This is evidence that even saints, especially young, fresh ones, may come unglued and lose their cool.

and blessed them while they were still in Europe. He gave them great strength when they fled from there, and for quite a few years he cared for them in the new land. He helped them overcome many Indian tribes and find a measure of security as the years passed. They had governors until the time of the Revolution, when they wanted their own rulers. God gave them Saul, and later David became President. Of David, God had these fine words to say: 'I have found David to be a man after my own heart, who will take seriously all my purposes.' Now just as God promised, he has raised up a descendant of David, a man named Jesus, to give freedom to this nation. John prepared the way for him by preaching that the entire nation should change its ways. In fact, while John was doing his thing, he said, "What do you think? That *I* am the one? No, indeed, but there *is* one coming after me whose shoes I am unworthy to shine."

26. "My brothers and fellow Americans who are serious about God, *we* have been let in on this idea of deliverance, even though the citizens of Atlanta, as well as their leaders, paid no attention to it nor the warnings of the Scriptures that are read in the church every Sunday. By condemning Jesus, they acted like the Bible said they would, and even though they could find no reason for killing him, they asked Pilate to give him the works. When they got through treating him as was to be expected, they took him down from the tree and buried him. But God made him alive again, and he was seen for a number of days by those who traveled with him from south Georgia to Atlanta, just as they are now telling the people about him. So it is, that we, too, are reminding you of the guarantee God made to our forefathers, and which he has made good on to us—their descendants—by raising up Jesus. It's like it says in Psalms 2: 'You are my boy; I myself fathered you for this day.' And when he said, 'I will restore to you David's dedication and David's faithfulness,' he was referring to raising Jesus from the dead, never again to be subjected to decay. In still another place it says, 'You won't let your special One die and rot.'

Now as for David, he did a good job for God in his own generation, but then he died, joined his departed relatives, and rotted.
But this One whom God raised did not rot. So let us make it clear
to you, my brothers, that through Jesus forgiveness of sins is being
offered to you, and anyone who accepts is cleared of all the things
he couldn't get free of under the old system of legalism. So make
sure that the warning spoken by the prophet doesn't apply to you:

'Look about you, you snobs, and get alarmed and get lost;
Because I am doing my thing in your own day,
A thing you wouldn't believe even if someone drew you
   a picture of it.' "

42. Afterwards, as they were leaving, people urged them to
come back next Sunday and tell them more about these things.
In fact, after the meeting had broken up, many prominent people
and active church workers followed Paul and Barney, who kept
on discussing with them and persuading them to hold tight to the
grace of God.

44. On the next Sunday, practically the whole town was there
to hear about God's "idea." But when the good white folks saw
such a crowd, they were eaten up with jealousy, and started arguing with Paul and smearing him. Paul and Barney, though, really
laid it on the line and said, "We felt obligated to explain God's
idea to you first, but since you cast it aside and don't consider
yourselves candidates for spiritual life, we're going over to the
outsiders, just as our Lord ordered us:

'I have put you as a light for the outsiders,
As a way of life for *all* mankind.' "

48. Upon hearing this, the outsiders were delighted and started
cheering for the Lord's idea. All who were prepared put their
faith in it, and the Lord's idea spread through the whole region.

50. The good white folks, however, got the Ladies Missionary Society and the town's leading men worked up, and they raised a big stink about Paul and Barney and ran them out of the city limits. Both of them told the crowd to go lump it, and then went on to Natchez. And the Lord's learners were just bubbling over with joy and Holy Spirit.

14.

1. At Natchez the very same thing happened when they went to a white church and spoke so convincingly that a whole lot of both whites and blacks got together in the Lord. But there were some stubborn whites who collared the blacks and filled their minds with vicious things about the brothers. So Paul and Barney stuck with it for a long time and spoke their minds about the Lord, who upheld the message of his undeserved favor by allowing them to do miraculous and wonderful things. But the town was split in two, some siding with the whites and some with the apostles. So when they found out that some whites and blacks had ganged up with the big shots to beat them up and lynch them, they hightailed it to Louisiana and started telling the good news in the area around Baton Rouge and New Orleans.

8. Now in Baton Rouge there was this crippled guy who had been born that way and never had walked. He was listening to Paul talking, and when Paul saw that he had the kind of faith to get well on, he looked him in the eye and shouted, "Get up on your feet like you're supposed to!" And the man jumped up and started walking around.

11. Well, when the people saw what Paul had done they buzzed with excitement. "They're Supermen!" they yelled. So they were calling Barney "Father Divine" and Paul "Elijah Mohammed," since he was the chief talker. The leading Black Muslim of the city brought money and other stuff, and wanted to hold a mass meeting. When the apostles, Barney and Paul, got wind of it they blew a gasket. They grabbed a bullhorn and said to the crowds, "Brothers, what in the world are you doing? We are just ordinary people like you, offering you the opportunity of turning away from all this junk to the living God who made land and sky and sea and all that's in them. Previously he let uncommitted people pretty much go their own way—although he never did withdraw himself entirely—but continued to do you good by sending from heaven rains and bountiful harvests, and by filling your hearts with nourishment and happiness." Even with such straight talk they could hardly keep the crowds from almost worshipping them.

19. But some good white folks came down from Vicksburg and Natchez, and got the people on their side. They beat the tar out of Paul and then dragged him out of town, leaving him for dead. While the Christians were hovering over him, he got up and re-entered the city. Next day he went with Barney to New Orleans. When they had spread the good news in that city and had made a lot of converts, they returned to Baton Rouge, Natchez and Vicksburg, putting some starch into the Lord's learners and encouraging them to stand firm in the faith. "We've got to put up with a lot of suffering," they said, "to get into the God Movement." They hand-picked some responsible leaders for each church, and after the ordination prayers they commended them to the Lord to whom they had committed their lives. They went all the way through Mississippi and came to Meridian, where they preached the Word. Then they went down to Hattiesburg and caught the bus back to Mobile, from which they had been set forward by God's grace for the task which they had accomplished.

27. Upon arriving, they called together the fellowship and reported on all the ways God had used them, and how he had opened the door of faith wide open to people of all races. They stayed on there with the Lord's learners for quite a spell.

125

15.

1. So, some folks from Georgia came down and started telling the brothers that unless they held on to the traditions they couldn't be Christians. Paul and Barney got into a terrific argument and hassle with them. So it was decided that Paul and Barney and several others from there should go up to Atlanta and talk with the original apostles and responsible leaders about this question. The church sent them on their way, and they went through north Florida and various Negro sections, making clear the membership of *all* races and bringing a lot of happiness to all the brothers. Upon their arrival in Atlanta they were given a warm welcome by the church and the original apostles and the responsible leaders. Then they recounted the various ways God had used them. But some church members who believed in segregation got up and said, "They've got to be told to accept segregation and all the traditional rules."

6. The apostles and leaders put their heads together to look into this idea. After a heated discussion, Rock got up and said to them, "Brothers, you yourselves are aware that way back at the beginning God selected me as the one among you to preach the Word to other races so they could hear and become faithful. And God, the heart-knower, openly supported them by giving them the Holy Spirit the same as he did to us. And when, through their faith, he straightened out their lives, he didn't make the slightest distinction between us and them. Now then, why are you trying God's soul by putting a load on the backs of the Lord's learners which neither we nor our daddies were able to tote? Instead, we believe that they, exactly the same as we, are saved by the undeserved favor of the Lord Jesus."

12. Nobody in the group said a word, and they paid close attention while Paul and Barney were recounting the marvelous and wonderful things God did among the Negroes through them. After

126

they got through talking, Jim said: "My brothers, listen to me, Simon has made clear just how God first looked around to find a group among the blacks to bear his Name. The words of the prophets fully support this when they say:

" 'Later on I'll return, and I will rebuild the dilapidated home of David;
I'll repair the things that have been vandalized, and completely remodel it,
That the dregs of society may search out the Lord,
And *all* races may claim my name for themselves,
Says the Lord who makes this clear from the beginning.'

"Therefore, I feel that we should not pester people from other races who are turning to God, but should advise them to steer clear of loose sex relations and to be extremely sensitive to and considerate of immature whites who have not outgrown their traditions,[7] since for generations these customs have been advocated on every Sabbath in every church throughout the South."

22. Then it occurred to the apostles and leaders, together with the whole fellowship, to appoint a committee to send to Mobile with Paul and Barney. They elected Joe, whom they called Barry, and Silas, men in whom the church had confidence, and wrote a letter which they sent by them. The letter said:

"Greetings from the apostles and church officers to our black brothers at Mobile and the rest of Alabama and Tennessee. Since we heard that some of us have stirred you up and pushed you around with ideas we never approved of, we agreed unanimously to appoint a committee and send them to you with our dear Barney and Paul, men whose lives are dedicated to our Lord Jesus Christ. We have, therefore, sent Joe and Silas, who will personally tell

[7]The literal translation here is: ". . . we should write to them to keep away from foods offered to idols, from fornication, from things strangled, and from blood," all of which were things particularly offensive to tradition-minded Hebrew-Christians.

you the same thing. For it occurred to the Holy Spirit and to us that we should not saddle you with any unnecessary burden other than that you be extremely sensitive to and considerate of immature whites who have not outgrown their traditions[8] and that you steer clear of loose sex relations. You'll be doing okay if you watch your step on these matters. Sincerely."

30. So they were sent on their way and went down to Mobile. There they called together the whole fellowship and delivered the letter. When the letter was read, the people were overjoyed by its encouragement. Then too, Joe and Silas, who were preachers themselves, encouraged and put starch into the brothers with a number of sermons. After they had spent some time there, they were given a warm send-off by the brothers and returned to their home church. Paul and Barney, however, stayed on in Mobile and joined with others in teaching and spreading the Lord's idea.

36. After a while Paul said to Barney, "Let's make another swing and drop in on the brothers in the various cities where we spread the Lord's idea and see how they're making out." Barney wanted to take John Mark with them again but Paul put his foot down. He wouldn't hear of taking along with them the guy who had deserted them in Mississippi and left them holding the bag. So they got into a knock-down, drag-out fight which ended in their separating from one another. Barney took Mark and caught the bus for South Carolina. Paul chose Silas and left after he was turned over to the Lord's grace by the brothers. He went through Alabama and Tennessee, pepping up the churches.

16.

1. Later, he headed for Baton Rouge and New Orleans. There he ran into a learner named Timothy, the son of a very devout

[8]See verse 20.

white woman, and whose father was a Negro. He was highly commended by the brothers in both Natchez and Baton Rouge. Paul
was anxious to have him travel with him even though it was common knowledge that his father was a Negro, so he got him baptized into a *white* church because there was so much tension in
that area. As they went from city to city they laid it on the members to stick by the decisions agreed upon by the original apostles
and the responsible leaders in Atlanta. As a result the churches
became more seasoned in the faith and their numbers were increasing daily.

6. So they traveled through Louisiana and Mississippi, but the
Holy Spirit wouldn't let them tell the idea in Texas. Then they
went on up into Missouri and thought about continuing to Kansas
but the Spirit of Jesus wouldn't let them go there either. So they
kept traveling through Missouri till they came to St. Louis. There
Paul had a vision one night; he saw a man from the North standing
and beckoning to him. "Come up North," the man said, "and give
us a hand." So right after this vision they were trying to go into the
North, confident that God had called them to spread the good news
among them.

11. Well, they left St. Louis and crossed the Mississippi, and
arrived the next day in Springfield, Ill. From there they went to
Chicago, which is one of the largest cities in the North and a very
important place. They decided to stop over there for a number of
days. One Sunday they went down by the side of the lake where
they got the impression a prayer meeting was held. They sat
around and got to talking with some of the ladies who had come
together. One lady named Lillian was a department store manager
from Evanston, and a very devout person. She listened carefully to
what Paul was saying and the Lord opened her heart to understand it. When she and her family were baptized, she extended an
invitation, saying: "If you have considered me to be loyal to the
Lord," she said, "please come and stay at my house."

129

16. One time on the way to prayer meeting they met this gal with the spirit of a whore who made a lot of money for her owners by practicing prostitution. She tagged along behind Paul and yelled, "These men are the servants of the Lord God Almighty. They're telling us how to be saved." This kept up over a long period. Finally Paul got a bellyful and turned to the spirit and said, "In the name of Jesus Christ I order you to come out of her." And it came out that instant! Now when her owners realized that she was ruined as a money-maker, they grabbed Paul and Silas and dragged them to the police station and turned them over to the cops. "These hoods are outside agitators who are causing a riot in our city! They're spreading communistic and un-American ideas!" The crowd got worked up against them, and the cops ripped their clothes and beat them with their billies. After the cops had pretty well loused them up, they threw them in the clink and told the jailer to make sure they didn't escape. When he got that order he put them in maximum security and chained their feet to the bars.

25. Along about midnight Paul and Silas were praying and singing some hymns, and the prisoners were listening intently to them. All of a sudden there was a big earthquake that shook the jailhouse foundations. Immediately all the cell doors were opened, and everybody's shackles fell off. When the jailer woke up and saw the jail doors wide open, he pulled his pistol and was about to shoot himself, assuming that all the prisoners had escaped. Then Paul shouted at the top of his voice, "Don't hurt yourself! We're all on deck!" Asking for a flashlight, the jailer went in, and trembling like a leaf, he got Paul and Silas and led them outside. "Sirs," he said, "what must *I* do to be liberated?" They told him, "Put your faith in the Lord Jesus, and you and your family will be liberated." And he explained the Lord's idea to him and his whole family. Even at that hour of the night, the jailer brought them and washed their wounds, while he himself and his family were baptized at once. He invited them over to his house and set

130

the table for them. He and the whole gang were as happy as a lark that he had put his faith in God.

35. When day came the judge sent word by the fuzzes to turn the men loose. The jailer greeted Paul with these words: "The judge has ordered you to be turned loose! Now you are free to go without any more trouble." But Paul replied, "They beat us publicly without a trial, denied our rights as American citizens, and threw us in the clink. And now they're kicking us out the back door? Not on your life! Let them come themselves and escort us out!" The cops went back and told the judge what had been said. They were all scared to death over the mention of rights as American citizens, so they came and pleaded with them, and escorted them out and begged them to please leave town. Paul and Silas then left the jail and went over to Lillian's house. When they had visited with the brothers and encouraged them, they took off.

17.

1. They made their way to South Bend and Toledo, and came to Cleveland, where there was a WAP[9] church. As was customary for Paul, he went there and for three straight Sundays he argued with them from the scriptures, bringing out and setting forth that the Christ[10] had to die and be raised from the dead. "This Head, whom I'm telling you about," he said, "is Jesus." Some of them were convinced and joined up with Paul and Silas. The same was true of a large group of devout blacks and of a good number of prominent women.

5. But the good white folks became incensed and picked up some lowdown bums off the street, formed a mob and started a riot in the city. They ransacked Jackson's house looking for Paul and

---

[9]White American Protestant.
[10]The divinely approved Head of the God Movement.

131

Silas so they could turn them over to the mob. Not finding them, they dragged Jackson and some brothers before the city authorities and howled, "These outside agitators have come here, and Jackson has housed them. All of them are going against the laws of the Federal Government, claiming that there's a higher authority named Jesus." Listening to this stuff terribly upset the crowd and the city authorities. They put Jackson and the others under bond and let them go.

10. At once the brothers sent Paul and Silas by night to Akron. Soon after arriving they attended a WAP church. Now the people in Akron were more open-minded than those in Cleveland, and they received the idea with great enthusiasm. They were studying the Bible every day to see if Paul was telling it like it is. The result was that many of them caught the idea, no small number of whom were prominent Negro men and women.

13. But when the good white folks from Cleveland found out that God's idea was now being set forth by Paul also in Akron, they came there and raised a big stink and got the crowds all worked up. The brothers then immediately sent Paul on a vacation while Silas and Tim were to stay there. Paul's escorts took him as far as Cincinnati, and returned with instructions to Silas and Tim to join him just at the earliest possible moment.

16. While Paul was waiting for them at Cincy he got sick at his stomach when he saw the city so full of chur h *buildings* of all denominations. So he got into dialogue with the good folks at the First WAP Church, and every day he handed out leaflets on the streets to passersby. Now some ministers of both liberal and conservative persuasion jumped him and said, "What's this gospel huckster trying to say? He seems to be a preacher of some very strange religion." (Paul was telling the good news that Jesus really was alive.) So they invited Paul to the Ministerial Association meeting and said, "We would like to know more about this new teaching of yours, for it surely sounds strange to us. We wish to know what it's all about." (Cincinnatians and their visitors, you know, do little else but discuss the latest fads and ideas.)

22. Paul then stood up before the Association and said, "Men of Cincinnati, I notice that in many ways you are extremely religious. For in going around and observing your sanctuaries, I even found one dedicated to 'The Unnamed God.' He whom you worship without naming, that's the one I'm telling you about. The God who made the universe and all that's in it, and who himself is Lord of land and sky, does not take up residence in a man-made sanctuary. Nor is he nourished by some handout from human beings, since he himself is the one who gives life and breath and everything else to all of us. It was he who made man, and from the one man, all the branches of humanity. He made it possible for them to live all over the world and he figured out and decided on when and where they were to flourish and live. He gave them a hunger for God, so they might grope for him and possibly find him, even though he is never very far from any one of us. For in him we come to life; in him we are motivated; in him we find meaning. As one of your own poets has put it:

'For we are indeed his stock.'

Since *we* are *God's* stock, we ought never to think of the Deity in terms of budgets or statistics or buildings—the product of man's craft and cunning. God used to excuse people when they didn't know better, but now he's making it clear to all people everywhere that they've got to change their ways. Because the appointed day is just about here when he'll judge the whole world on the *justice* they've done as measured by the Man whom he selected and validated, by raising him from the dead."

32. When they heard the bit about the "resurrection from the dead," some of them just hee-hawed, but others said, "We would like to hear more about this some time." That's the way it was when Paul left them. Some people did join up, though, and catch the idea, among whom were Dickerson, the secretary, and a lady named Doris, and several others.

18.

1. After this Paul left Cincy and went to Louisville. There he met a Jew named Abrams, a native of Bavaria, with his wife, Priscilla, who had come to this country from Germany when Hitler ran all the Jews out of Berlin. Paul went over to their house and stayed with them, and since they had the same trade they worked together. (They were electricians by trade.) Every Sunday he held a discussion at the church to which he invited both whites and blacks.

5. Now when Silas and Tim arrived from up North, Paul was eaten up with the idea and laid it out plain to the white folks that Jesus is the Head. But when they objected and smeared him, he washed his hands of them and said, "Okay, let your guilt be nobody's but your own! I'm no longer responsible. From here on out I'm walking with the blacks." And he left there and went to the house of a dedicated Negro man named Tyler Justice, who lived next to the church. Reverend Crisp, the pastor of the church, and his whole family, had faith in the Lord, as did a number of Louisville people, and they were baptized.

9. One night Paul had a vision in which the Lord said, "Don't be scared, but say your piece and don't pull in your horns, because I'm in this with you. Nobody is going to lift a finger to hurt you, for there's a big group for me in this city." So he stayed on there a year and a half, teaching them God's idea.

12. During the time that Gelston was a district judge in Kentucky, the white folks organized against Paul, took him to court

134

and prosecuted him on the grounds that "this man is getting people to break the law in the name of religion." Paul was about to speak in his defense when the judge said to the plaintiffs: "If this were a matter involving some illegal act or punishable crime, gentlemen, I would patiently hear your case. But if it is a question of theology and name-calling and religious bickering, you must settle it among yourselves. I refuse to rule on such matters." And he dismissed the case. They then jumped on the Reverend Sam Thomas, pastor of the church, and beat him up right there in the courtroom. And Judge Gelston would get involved no further with the affair.

18. After Paul had stayed on some days longer, he told the brothers good-bye and took a bus for Alabama. Abrams and Priscilla went with him. (He got a haircut in Bowling Green, for he had made a promise.) They arrived in Nashville and he left them there. He himself went to a church and got into a discussion with the whites. And even though they asked him to stay longer with them, he wouldn't hear of it. Telling them good-bye, he said, "Another day, God willing, I'll return to you." So he left Nashville and came to Birmingham. He went over to the church, and after greeting them he set out for Mobile. He spent a good bit of time there and then left again, making a swing through Mississippi and Louisiana, putting muscle on all the Lord's learners.

25. Now a white fellow named Oliver, a native of Jacksonville, arrived in Nashville. He was a fine speaker and a powerful Bible student. Well-taught himself in the Lord's Way, and spiritually aglow, he was speaking and teaching very accurately all that he knew about Jesus. His knowledge, however, went only up to the baptism by John. He began to be quite outspoken in the church, and when Abrams and Priscilla heard him they took him aside and explained for him God's Way in greater detail. He was anxious to go to Kentucky, so the brothers gave him a hand and wrote a letter of recommendation to the Lord's learners there.

When he arrived, he was a big boost to those who, by God's undeserved favor, had become pilgrims of the Way. For he vigorously confronted the WAPs in public with proof from the Bible that Jesus is Head of the Movement.

19.

1. While Oliver was in Louisville, Paul headed northward till he came again to Birmingham. He found some learners there, and he asked them "when you came over to the faith, did you get Holy Spirit?" They said, "We heard no mention of Holy Spirit." "Then into what were you initiated?" "Into John's initiation." Paul replied, "John's initiation was a symbol of the changed life and he told the people that they may confidently trust in the one who would succeed him, that is, in Jesus." On getting this information, they were initiated into the name of the Lord Jesus. And when Paul put his hands on them, the Holy Spirit came over them and they began tongue-talking and preaching. There were about a dozen men in all.

8. For a period of three months he attended a WAP church and in both discussions and debates he came on strong for the God Movement. But some of them turned up their noses, acted mean, and hurled abuse at the Way, in front of the crowds, so Paul parted company with them, withdrew his students, and went over to Birmingham-Southern College where he held discussions every day. This continued for about two years until the people of Alabama, both whites and blacks, heard the Lord's idea.

11. God was powerfully using Paul to do tremendous things. For example, bandannas and blue jeans which he had used were taken to the sick, and their illnesses were cured and the mean spirits left them.

13. Well, there was this team of traveling faith healers who made a try at using the Lord Jesus' name on people who had mean spirits. "I order you out in the name of the Jesus that Paul talks about," was their formula. (The men doing this were the seven sons of a white bishop by the name of Stevens.) But the mean-spirited man answered, "I know Jesus, and I'm acquainted with Paul, but who in hell are you?" With that, the mean-spirited man jumped all over them, pinned them down and beat the tar out of them. They escaped from the building with their clothes torn to shreds and bloody all over. News of this spread throughout Birmingham to whites and blacks alike. Everybody was pretty well shook up, and they had great respect for the name of the Lord Jesus. Many who believed came forward, publicly admitting and making a clean breast of their actions. A large number of hate-mongers brought their literature and burned it in front of everybody. They tallied up the value of it and it came to ten thousand dollars. With this kind of authority the Lord's idea spread and held sway.

21. It was after this that Paul decided to swing through the North again, back down to Kentucky and from there to Atlanta. "And then," he said, "I've got to visit Washington." So he sent two of his assistants, Tim and Ernest, up North, but he himself stayed on a while in Alabama. About that time a big hullabaloo regarding the Way broke out in Birmingham. A guy named De Mille, a contractor, who specialized in building churches and shrines, had some highly paid craftsmen whom, with other members of the union, he got worked up about what was going on. "Men, you realize that we make our living from this business," he said. "Now you can see and hear for yourselves, not only in Birmingham but throughout almost all of Alabama, that this Paul is persuading a lot of people to turn away. He is teaching that man-made buildings are not houses of God. By doing this, he not only casts a reflection on the union, but there is a real danger that he will completely discredit the Cathedral of the Blessed Holy

Mother and destroy her preeminence—she who is respected in Alabama and the whole world."

28. Well, when they heard that, they blew a fuse and started shouting, "Blessed be the Holy Mother!" The whole city got embroiled in the controversy and they paraded to the park, dragging along two Yankees, Barry and Stocky, who were Paul's buddies. Paul wanted to address the mob, but his brothers wouldn't let him. Besides, some of the commissioners who were his friends sent word to him urging him to stay away from the park. All the while the mob was shouting first one thing and then another. There was such confusion that hardly any of them knew why they had come together. Someone in the crowd called for Alexander, who was a spokesman for the Protestants, to make a speech. Alexander motioned to the mob and tried to speak to them. But when they learned that he was a WAP, they shouted him down in union, and for a space of about two hours they chanted, "Blessed be the Holy Mother."

35. The city attorney finally quieted them down and said, "Citizens of Birmingham, is there anyone who is not aware of the reverence of this city for the Holy Mother and for the cathedral erected in her honor? Since nobody contradicts this, you ought to settle down now and do nothing foolish. For you have jumped on these men who are neither burners of churches nor smearers of our religion. So then, if De Mille and the union have a charge against anybody, the courts are available and there are judges; let them take their complaints there. Right now we are dangerously close to a riot. There's no excuse for this and we simply can't defend this senseless uproar!" With that he dispersed the crowd.

20.

1. After the excitement died down, Paul called together the fellowship, and when he had reassured them he told them goodbye and left to go West. He traveled all through those parts and spoke the good word to them. Then he went to Texas and spent three months there. Just as he was about to leave for Alabama, the WAPs cooked up a plot against him, and when he got wind of it he headed towards the North. In the party by now were Searcy Powell, a native of Akron; Stocky and Seymour from Cleveland; Garry and Tim from New Orleans; and Tic and Troy from Alabama. They all went on ahead and waited for the rest of us in St. Louis. After Thanksgiving we caught a bus in Houston and joined them in St. Louis where we stayed a week. On Sunday night we all gathered for a church supper, and Paul spoke. He kept going until midnight since he was planning to leave next day. It was hot and stuffy in the upstairs room where we were meeting. A young fellow named Eubanks was sitting in the window, and while Paul preached on and on, he dozed off and fell sound asleep. He was really sawing wood when all of a sudden he fell out the window to the ground three stories below. He was dead when we got to him. But Paul rushed down, knelt beside him and put his arms around him. "Don't y'all get upset," he said, "he's still breathing." Then Paul went back upstairs, fixed a sandwich and ate it, began a lengthy discussion that lasted till daybreak, and then left. Those in the party took the boy, Eubanks, home alive, and were thrilled no end about that.

13. Now Paul told us to go ahead of him and catch the bus for Litchfield, since he would be coming there but planned to walk. When he joined us at Litchfield, we went on up to Springfield and from there to Peoria. The next day we went to LaSalle and then to Joliet. Paul thought it best to bypass Chicago so he wouldn't waste a lot of time in traffic. He was anxious to get to Atlanta if at all possible by the Christmas holidays. So he phoned from Joliet for the church leaders in Chicago to meet him down there. When they arrived, he said to them, "You all are fully aware of my conduct all the while I was with you from the very first day I was in Illinois. With a humble mind I enslaved myself to the

139

Lord in the midst of the sorrows and trials that came my way from the plots of the WAPs. I didn't hesitate to tell you anything that might benefit you, as I taught you both publicly and privately. Before whites and blacks alike I stood for the changed life under God and complete trust in our Lord Jesus. And now listen, I feel spiritually compelled to go to Atlanta. Just what will happen to me there I do not know, except that wherever I turn the Holy Spirit makes it clear to me that jail and trouble are waiting for me. But I put no value at all on my life, so as to make good at my job and appointment which I got from the Lord Jesus, that is, being an example of the good news of God's undeserved favor. And now listen, I realize that you all among whom I've gone around telling about the Movement will never see me again. So I want to go on record that I am no longer responsible for you all, for I have never hesitated to lay before you God's total purpose. Keep an eye on yourselves, as well as on the whole group over which the Holy Spirit made you guardians. Take good care of God's fellowship, which He has brought together around the death of his Son. I'm convinced that after my departure greedy wolves will come among you who won't have the slightest concern for the fellowship. Even from your own ranks there will arise men who will distort the truth just to get the Christians to come over to their camp. So really stay on your toes, remembering that night and day I never stopped nourishing you with tender concern. And now I'm turning you over to the Lord and to the idea of his undeserved favor—the idea that's capable of expanding you and giving you the inheritance which falls to the committed. I haven't wanted anybody's money or car or clothes. You yourselves know that these hands of mine provided for my needs and for those of the others with me. In every way I made it plain to you that the strong should work like that and give a hand to the weak, keeping in mind the words of the Lord Jesus when he said, "It is more noble to share than to get."

36. When he had finished, he knelt down with the whole group and prayed. Everybody started crying their eyeballs out as they put their arms around Paul and kissed him and kissed him. What made them especially sad were his words that they would never see him again. Then they took him to the bus station.

21.

1. The bus pulled out and we left them, making the first stop at Gary, the next one at Plymouth and from there we went to Ft. Wayne, where we changed buses and got on one going to Columbus. We barely missed Kentucky on the way to Charleston, West Virginia, where the bus unloaded a lot of baggage. We looked up some of the brothers there and decided to stop over with them for a week. They too, under the leadership of the Spirit, warned Paul not to continue to Atlanta. But when our visit was over, we packed up to leave and all of them, even the women and children, went with us to the bus station. After a period of prayer together, we got on the bus and they returned to their homes.

7. When our bus left Charleston, we made it to Columbia, S.C., and stopped over a day to greet the brothers there. Next day we left for Augusta, and on arriving we were taken to the home of Philip the missionary (one of the original seven deacons), where we stayed. Philip had four unmarried daughters who were ministers. While we were spending some time there a preacher by the name of Albert arrived from Georgia. He came by to see us, and taking Paul's belt he tied himself hand and foot and said, "Here's what the Holy Spirit is saying: 'The white folks in Atlanta are going to tie up the owner of this belt and hand him over to a mob.' " Well, when we heard that, we and the local people practically got down on our knees to keep Paul from going on to Atlanta. But his reply was, "What do you mean crying and tearing my heart out? For I am prepared not only to go to jail in Atlanta but also to die for the name of our Lord Jesus." Unable to persuade him, we resigned ourselves and said, "Let the Lord's will run its course."

15. After a few days we packed up and left for Atlanta, accompanied by some of the Augusta members. They took us to the home of a very early Christian, a man from Kentucky named Manson, who was to be our host. The brothers in Atlanta received us joyfully when we got there.

18. Next day Paul and we had an appointment with Jim, who was joined by all the church leaders. After Paul had greeted them, he explained point by point how God had used him to reach the blacks. They praised God for what they heard, but they said, "You can see for yourself, brother, how many thousands of white Southerners have joined the church, and they are all on fire for the old time religion. Now they have been warned about you, that you are teaching people in other parts of the country to disregard the Bible, not to keep their children segregated, and to go contrary to our customs. Surely they're going to hear that you've come, and then what? Well, here's what we advise you to do. There are four men here who are candidates for baptism. Take them to church with you during the revival, give them some money for the offering, and do all you can to prepare them for baptism. Then everybody will know that there's nothing to the warnings they got about you, but that you really do stand for all the old time religion. We might say, however, regarding the Negro converts, we did send them a letter urging them to be extremely sensitive to and considerate of immature whites who have not outgrown their traditions, and to avoid loose sex relations."[11] Then Paul took the men to the revival next day, told how he was giving them candidates' instruction, and when they expected to be baptized.

29. Just as the week of revival was about to end, some WAPs from Alabama spied him in the church and whipped up the people

---

[11]See Chapter 15: 20, 28.

against him. They grabbed hold of him and shouted, "Fellow Southerners, help us. This is the man who turns people everywhere against good white folks and the Bible and the church. And worse, he has even brought a nigger into the church and broke up our fine spirit of Christian unity and fellowship." (For they had previously seen Troy, a Negro from Chicago, in town with him and had assumed that Paul had taken him to the revival too.) The whole crowd got excited and a mob started forming. They jumped Paul, dragged him out of the sanctuary, and then the doors were locked. They were giving Paul the works when somebody phoned the police that there was about to be a riot in Atlanta. Right away the chief got some cops and rushed to the scene. When they saw the chief and the cops they quit beating on Paul. Then the chief came over, arrested him, and ordered him to be handcuffed. He began inquiring who he was and what he had done, but some of the mob yelled one thing and others another. Because of the ruckus, the chief couldn't find out anything definite, so he ordered Paul to be taken to city hall. They started up the steps with him but the crowd was so violent that the cops had to protect him. The whole bunch was hot after him, screaming, "Kill him."

37. They were about to go into city hall when Paul said to the chief, "Please let me have a word with you." "So, you have a Southern accent," the chief said. "Then you're not the Yankee agitator who started that riot in Memphis?" Paul said, "I'm a native Southerner, from Tallahassee, Florida, a very reputable city. Now I beg you, let me speak to the crowd." The chief agreed, so Paul stood on the steps and motioned to the people for silence. When they quieted down, he began talking to them in his Southern accent:

22.

1. "My brothers and fathers, gentlemen: please listen carefully to me now as I explain my position." When they heard that he

143

had a Southern accent they listened all the more quietly. He continued, "I am a Southerner, born in Tallahassee, Florida, but reared in this city. I was graduated from Georgia Tech and was about as straitlaced, dyed-in-the-wool WAP as any of you here today. In fact, I was one of the ring leaders of those trying to stamp out this Way, trumping up charges against both men and women, as the White Citizens Council will affirm. Indeed, the officers supplied me with warrants and I was going to Chattanooga to arrest the brothers there and bring them bound to Atlanta for sentencing. Well, it so happened that when I stopped about noon on the outskirts of Chattanooga, all of a sudden a brilliant light from the sky engulfed me. I fell to the pavement, and heard a voice saying to me 'Saul! Saul! Why are you so mean to me?' And I answered, 'Who are you, sir?' Then he said to me, 'I am Jesus from Valdosta, whom you're harassing.' (Now the fellows who were with me saw the light, but they didn't understand what was said to me.) 'What shall I do, sir?' I asked. And the Lord said to me, 'Get up now and go on in to Chattanooga, and there you'll be informed of all that's been mapped out for you.' Because I was blinded by the brightness of the light, the fellows with me had to lead me till I got to Chattanooga. Well, there was this guy named Harry, a Southerner from an old-line family, as any of the white people around there can tell you, and he came and stood up to me and said, 'Saul, brother, look up.' And at that very moment I looked up at him. 'The God of our founding fathers,' he said, 'has selected you to understand his purpose, to meet his Just One, and to hear his message straight from his mouth; because you are to be a faithful witness to all mankind of the things which you experience. So, what's the next step now? Come on, be initiated, scrub off your sins, and identify yourself as a Christian.'

17. "When I went back to Atlanta I had a vision while I was praying at the church. I saw Him as he spoke to me, 'Don't waste a minute getting out of Atlanta right now, because they're not going to tolerate your faithfulness to me.' And I said, 'But Lord, they themselves fully understand that I was going from church to church arresting and beating those who walked in your way. And when your faithful Stephen was lynched, I myself was standing there, giving my approval and holding their coats while they did him in.' But he said to me, 'Get moving, because I will make you a friend of blacks.' "

22. They were listening to him until he said that word, and then they began screaming, "Send him back to Russia! He's got no right to live here!" While they were yelling bloody murder, working themselves into a lather and throwing pop bottles, the chief ordered Paul to be taken into city hall and told some of the cops to work him over to see if they could find out just why the mob was after his hide. As they were getting ready to do this, Paul asked an officer who was standing there, "Is it lawful to deny an American citizen his constitutional rights before you've even tried him?" At that the officer went to the chief and said, "You'd better be careful what you do, because this cat's talking about his 'constitutional rights.' " So the chief went to him and said, "Tell me, are you thinking about taking this into the Federal courts?" He said, "I certainly am." And the chief said, "It costs an awful lot of money to fight for 'constitutional rights.' " To which Paul replied, "But they are mine by birth!" So right away those who were about to work him over left off. And the chief was scared because he had arrested Paul and he might get involved in the Federal court.

30. The chief wanted to know just what to charge Paul with, so the next day he called together some of the leading citizens, including the bishop, and brought Paul from his cell and stood him before them.

23.

1. Paul looked them in the eye and said, "Gentlemen and brothers, to this very day I have lived my life before God with a

145

clear conscience." Bishop Harry told those standing near Paul to slap him. Then Paul said to him, "God will slap you, you damned hypocrite! You're sitting there passing judgment on my orthodoxy and in an unorthodox manner you order me to be slapped?" Somebody next to Paul asked him, "Are you insulting God's bishop?" Paul replied, "I was unaware, brothers, that he was a bishop. For the Bible says, 'You must not cuss an official of your church.' "

6. Paul noticed that some in the group were Unitarians and some were Baptists, so he called out: "Gentlemen and brothers, I myself am a Baptist, the son of a Baptist. I am being tried on the issue of whether there is hope and newness of life for the dead." When he said this, the Baptists and the Unitarians started feuding, and the group was split. (For the Unitarians don't believe in the resurrection or angels or the spirit, while the Baptists believe in all of them.) There was a monstrous hubbub. Some of the Baptist preachers jumped up and loudly asserted: "We see nothing bad in this fellow. Maybe an angel spoke to him, or a spirit." It looked like the argument was reaching the knock-down, drag-out stage, and the chief was afraid they would pull Paul apart. So he told the cops to go in and rescue him and take him back to city hall.

11. On the next night the Lord stood beside Paul and said, "Keep your chin up, because you've got to stand up for me in Washington just as you have here in Atlanta."

12. A day later the Klan hatched a plot, swearing to themselves that they wouldn't eat or drink till they had lynched Paul. There were more than forty of them in on this deal. They went to some of the local bigwigs and said, "Look, we've sworn not to eat anything till we've gotten rid of that Paul. Now you all try to arrange another hearing for him as though you wanted to get more information, and have the chief bring him over to the court house. We'll be ready to gun him down on the way over."

146

16. But the son of Paul's sister overhead the plot, went to the city jail and told Paul about it. Paul called one of the guards and said, "Take this young fellow to the chief; he has something to tell him." The guard then took him to the chief. "That prisoner, Paul," he said, "called and asked me to bring this young fellow to you. Says he has something to tell you." The chief took him by the hand, went aside privately with him and asked, "What is it you want to tell me?" The youth said, "The Klan has plotted to ask you to bring Paul to the courthouse tomorrow as though there would be another hearing on his case. But don't you let them trick you into it, because there are more than forty men in on the deal and they've sworn they won't eat or drink anything till they've wiped him out. They're ready right now, just waiting for you to give your permission." The chief then let the boy go. "But don't you dare tell a soul," he warned, "that you have tipped me off."

23. He then rang for two of his lieutenants. "Get your squads ready to go to Augusta at nine o'clock tonight. Be prepared for anything, and have a special car to take Paul in and to see that he gets to Federal Judge Felton." He wrote a letter along this line:
"From Claud Lyman, to His Honor, Judge Felton, greetings: This man fell into the hands of a white mob that was about to lynch him. Being aware that he has certain constitutional rights, I sent my men to rescue him. Wanting to find out what charge they had against him, I took him before a meeting of them. But I found they were mad at him because of some religious matters of their own, and that there were no valid legal charges to bring against him. Then when I got wind of a plot against the man, I immediately sent him to you and told his accusers to lay their case before you."

31. The policemen carried out their orders. That night they took Paul as far as Athens. The next day the squad car went on with him, and the others returned to Atlanta. Upon arriving in Augusta they delivered the letter to the judge and turned Paul over to him. The judge read the letter, and asked what state the prisoner was from. Being informed that Paul was from Florida, he said, "I'll hear your case when your accusers arrive." He ordered him to be held in the Federal jail.

24.

1. Five days later Bishop Harry and some church officials,[12] along with a lawyer named Turner, showed up to press the charges against Paul before the judge. When court convened, Turner was called upon to present the charges. He said: "Your honor, because of you we are enjoying law and order, and through your wise counsel many worthwhile changes have come about. For this we are abundantly and unceasingly grateful. But lest I weary you further, I'll get down to brass tacks, asking that you hear me with your usual patience. For our investigation shows that this man—this public pest—incites riots among the good white folks wherever he goes, and that he is a spark plug in the Valdostan gang. He was disturbing divine worship, so we arrested him. When you examine him, you'll be able to tell for yourself that all these charges we have against him are true." The white folks backed him up, claiming that he had accurately presented the facts.

10. The judge now nodded to Paul to speak, and he began: "Knowing that you have had long experience as a judge in this district, I gladly lay the facts of my case before you. As you can easily find out, it has been no more than twelve days since I went to Atlanta to worship. But they never found me arguing in the

---

[12]It must be kept in mind that the Jewish religious leaders had both civil and ecclesiastical authority, so we have no modern counterpart for them. Likewise the Roman governors and kings held both judicial and executive powers, and we have no one on the American scene to represent them. Therefore, since the first century, legal, political and ecclesiastical structures were so unlike ours, it is impossible to put them in the "cotton patch" perspective with any degree of accuracy.

church sanctuary or causing a public disturbance, either in the churches or in the streets. Nor are they able to prove to you the charges they now have against me. I do admit this to you, however, that I serve our Father-God as a member of what they call a 'gang.' I believe in the Bible from cover to cover. I have a confidence in God which they themselves support—that he will raise both the just and the unjust. I constantly give myself workouts in this so as to have a clear conscience toward God and my fellow-man.

17. "Having been away for some years, I had the desire to return, and to make an offering and go to worship with my own people. While doing this, I was sitting quietly in the sanctuary. I had no crowd; I created no commotion. But I was set upon by some hoods from Alabama, who should be present now, and present their charges to you if they have anything against me. Or for that matter, let these gentlemen right here state what they found me guilty of when I appeared before the Council—unless perhaps it was for this one statement I made as I stood before them: 'I am being tried before you today on the issue of newness of life for the dead.' "

22. Then Judge Felton, who had some inside dope on the Way, recessed court. "When Chief Lyman comes," he said, "I'll hear you further on this case." He ordered the marshal to keep him in custody, but to grant him every privilege and to let his friends visit and wait on him.

24. Some time later, Judge Felton and his wife, Drusilla, a member of the DAR, sent for Paul to hear him talk about the Christian faith. But when Paul got on the subject of justice, integrity and eternal judgment, Judge Felton got scared and said, "I've had enough for now; you may go. When I have another opportunity, I'll call you again." All the while, though, he was hoping that Paul would offer him a bribe. This was the real reason he fetched him so often and chatted with him.

149

27. Two years passed, and "Porky" Foster succeeded Judge Felton. Wishing to please the good white folks, Felton left Paul in jail.

25.

1. Three days after Foster took office, he went to Atlanta from Augusta. There some influential WAPs brought up the subject of Paul and tried to get Judge Foster to do them a favor by summoning Paul to Atlanta for trial. (They had a scheme to kill him on the way there.) But Judge Foster's answer was: "Paul is being kept in Augusta, and I myself plan to return there soon. Let your lawyers go over there with me, and if he has done something illegal, let them press the charges against him."

6. He spent no more than eight or ten days with them and returned to Augusta. The next day he convened court and ordered Paul's case to be called. During the proceedings, the whites who had come from Atlanta leveled many serious accusations against him, but they couldn't make them hold any water. In making his defense, Paul denied that he had committed any crime against the laws and customs of local whites, against the church, or against the Federal government. But Judge Foster, with an eye to making himself popular with the good white folks, asked Paul, "Would you be willing to go to Atlanta and let me hear your case there?" Paul replied, "I am standing in a Federal court right now, where I should be tried. I have done no harm to the white people, as you yourself know beyond all doubt. If indeed I have broken a law, or committed some crime punishable even by death, I ask for no mercy. But if there's no basis for the things these people are charging me with, nobody can let them put their cotton picking hands on me! I'm appealing to the Supreme Court!"

12. Judge Foster then conferred with his associates, and gave Paul an answer. "You have appealed to the Supreme Court. To the Supreme Court you shall go."

150

13. Well, the days passed and Governor Griffin and his wife Bernice went to Augusta to pay their respects to Judge Foster. After they had visited a while, Judge Foster mentioned Paul's case to the Governor. "You know, there's a fellow here who was left in jaid by Felton, and when I went to Atlanta, some influential whites approached me about him and asked that I sentence him. But I told them that it is not constitutional to sentence any accused person before he has had his day in court, and has been confronted with his accusers. So when they got together here, I made no postponement. The very next day I convened court and ordered the fellow to be brought in. The plaintiffs stated their case, but they presented no evidence of the crime which I had presumed. Instead, they had only disputes with him about their own religious doctrines and about some Jesus guy who had died and whom Paul swore was still alive. Being in doubt as to how to proceed on such matters, I asked Paul if he would be willing to go to Atlanta and stand trial there concerning them. But he chose to appeal to the Supreme Court for a decision, so I ordered him to be held until I could send him there." Governor Griffin said to Judge Foster, "I'd like a chance to hear the man myself." "Okay," he said, "you shall hear him tomorrow."

23. So Governor Griffin and Bernice arrived next day with a great show and entered the court room. With them were some high brass and government dignitaries of the city. Judge Foster ordered Paul to be brought in, and said, "Governor Griffin and all you gentlemen present with us, this man you see here is the one about whom a lot of good white folks have approached me both in Atlanta and here. They yell to high heaven, claiming he shouldn't be allowed to live any longer. But my investigation showed that he had committed no capital crime and so when he appealed to the Supreme Court, I granted it. Yet I have nothing specific about him to present to them. The reason then that I have brought him before you all, and especially before you, Governor Griffin, is that on the basis of this inquiry I might have something to present. For

151

it seems ridiculous to me to send a prisoner without stating the charges against him."

26.

1. So Governor Griffin said to Paul, "You may now state your own position." Then Paul raised his hand and began his defense:

"In regard to everything of which I am accused by white people, Governor Griffin, I consider it a privilege to make my defense today before you, especially since you are well acquainted with the various customs and beliefs of white American Protestants. Please, then, listen patiently to me.

"All the whites are acquainted with my past—that I was brought up as a kid in Atlanta among my own people. They have known all along, if they would but speak up, that I was reared a Baptist, one of the most orthodox Protestant sects. And now I'm being condemned for having confidence in the guarantee which God made with our forefathers, a guarantee which our whole denomination pins its hopes on during its round of activities. For such confidence, Governor, I am damned—by white Christians! Why do you all consider it heresy to believe that God raises the dead?

"Indeed, I myself thought I should do all I could to stop the Jesus movement. And so I got right to work in Atlanta. I was appointed as a deputy by the authorities, and personally jailed a number of the members. Not only that, but when they were killed, I voted in favor of it. Many a time I even went into the churches and put the heat on them trying to make them chuck it all. I was so terribly brain-washed that I hunted them down in the outlying cities. On one such mission I was going to Chattanooga at the request of the authorities, and about noon, Your Excellency, I saw a light more brilliant than the sun coming from the sky and shining on me and those traveling with me. We all fell on the pavement and I heard a voice saying to me with a Southern accent, 'Saul! Saul! Why are you so mean to me? It's rough on you when you take the bit in your own teeth.' And I said, 'Who are you, sir?' Then the Lord said, 'I am Jesus whom you're harassing. But get up and stand on your own two legs. Now here's why I've appeared to you: I have selected you to be a trustee and a faithful witness of what you're seeing now and of what I'll show you in the future. I'm singling you out from your own people and from other races, to whom I'm sending you. You are to open their eyes, to face them from the darkness toward the light, and from Satan's authority to God's; to take them freedom from wrongs and an inheritance among those who have been set apart by a faith rooted in me.'

19. "So then, Governor Griffin, I was not callous to the spiritual encounter. Instead, I began telling the people first in Chattanooga and Atlanta, and later through all the country—both whites and blacks—to reshape their lives and face toward God, backing it up with actions which follow a changed life. It was for this, sir, that the whites grabbed me in the sanctuary and tried to tear me to pieces. But I took hold of God's hand, and to this very day I stand, telling it straight to both high and low. I'm saying nothing but what the Bible has said all along—that the Leader[13] would be killed, that he as the first of a raising of the dead, would herald the dawn to people of all races."

24. At this point in Paul's argument, Judge Foster loudly interrupted, "You're nuts, Paul. Too much education has driven you nutty." Paul replied, "Most honorable Judge Foster, I am *not* nuts. I am but speaking the sober truth. The Governor understands these things. I can discuss them freely with him, for I am convinced that not one of these things has escaped his memory. After all, it's no deep, dark secret! Governor Griffin, you believe the Bible, don't you? Of course you believe it." But Griffin said to Paul, "You are trying to get me to be a Christian with a minority!" Paul said, "I wish to God, whether in a minority or in a ma-

---

[13]Or the Messiah, or the Christ.

153

jority, not only you but all the people who are listening to me today were in my situation—except for being in jail."

30. The Governor, the judge, Bernice and those sitting with them got up and as they went out they were discussing it among themselves. "This fellow isn't doing a thing that deserves either death or a jail term," they said. And Governor Griffin told Foster, "This man could be turned loose if he hadn't appealed to the Supreme Court."

27.

[At this point, and continuing through 28:15, we return with Paul to the original setting in the first century. This passage is simply a travelogue of Paul's journey to Rome (Washington). To put it in a modern setting and remain within even remote range of the text would not only be well nigh impossible, but would add little or nothing to an understanding of it. By making the trip with Paul aboard the ancient sailing vessel, we'll probably get more "feel" for it than if we were flying with him on a twentieth century jet. At least we'll breathe a wee bit easier through the "wreck" episode!]

1. Now when the decision was made to ship us out for Italy, Paul and some other prisoners were put in the custody of a Captain Julius of the Emperor's Corps. With Aristarchus, from Thessalonica, Macedonia, we boarded a ship from Adramyttium which was heading for various places in Asia, and set sail. The next day we put into Sidon. Now Julius treated Paul like a human being and let him contact his friends to get what items he needed. We pulled out of there and, due to the head winds, we sailed behind Cyprus, then across the sea opposite Cilicia and Pamphylia until we came to Myra, Lycia. The captain located an Alexandrian boat there which was sailing for Italy, so he loaded us on it. For several days we inched along and just barely made it to Cnidus. Unable to continue against the wind, we sailed around Salmone and down behind Crete. We stayed close to shore and had a real rough time making it to a place called Fair Havens, near the city of Lasea on the island of Crete.

9. A lot of time had gotten away from us and it was already dangerous to sail, since it was past Thanksgiving. Paul cautioned them, "Men, it's clear to me that if you continue the voyage it will result in much damage and loss not only to the cargo and ship but to us as well." But Captain Julius was influenced more by the skipper and the ship owner than by Paul's advice. And since it wasn't a suitable harbor for wintering in, the majority favored getting out and trying to make it to Phoenix, to winter there. It's a harbor on Crete that faces southwest and northwest.

13. When the wind started blowing from the south, they thought they had it made, so they weighed anchor and sailed along just off the shore of Crete. It wasn't long, though, till Hurricane Euraquilla hit her. It lashed the boat so hard that we couldn't head her into the wind, so we gave up and were swept along. When we ran behind a little island called Clauda we managed, with great difficulty, to make the lifeboat secure. We pulled it on board and used some ropes to lash it to the ship. They were afraid they might run aground on the Syrtis sand banks, so they hauled down the mainsail and let her drift. On the next day we were taking an awful beating from the storm, and they dumped the cargo overboard. The day following they tore loose with their bare hands the ship's furnishings. Neither sun nor stars shone for days on end, and with no small hurricane pounding us, we finally gave up all hope of surviving.

21. After they had gone several days without food, Paul then said to them as they huddled together, "Fellows, you should have followed my advice and never left Crete, and we wouldn't have

155

had all this damage and loss. But now forget it and keep your chins up. Not a man of you will lose his life, but we will lose the ship. For last night there stood beside me an angel of the God to whom I belong and to whom I give my allegiance, and he said to me, 'Don't let this scare you, Paul, because you've got to appear before Caesar. Now listen, God has made it possible for the whole company to come through with you.' So brighten up, fellows; I trust God to do exactly as he told me. However, we've got to be wrecked on some island."

27. About midnight of the fourteenth day, as we were being driven along in the Adriatic, the sailors had a hunch that we were approaching land. So they sank a line and found that the depth was twenty fathoms (120 feet). They waited a little while and sank the line again. This time it was fifteen fathoms (90 feet). Fearing that we might be cast up on a jagged shore, they threw out four anchors from the stern and kept their fingers crossed, hoping for daylight.

30. Now the sailors tried to escape from the ship by lowering the lifeboat into the sea and pretending that they were going to put out anchors from the ship. But Paul said to the captain and the guards, "Unless these men stay with the ship, you all can't be saved." Then the guards cut the lifeboat's ropes and let her drift.

33. Just before dawn Paul urged everybody to eat something. "You have been on duty fourteen days today," he said, "and you've gone without food all that time. So come on now, y'all eat something. You'll need the strength to get through this alive, for not a one of you is going to lose a hair on his head." After saying this, he took a loaf of bread, gave thanks in front of everybody, broke off a chunk and began eating it. They all grinned and began digging in themselves. (There were two hundred and seventy-six of us on the ship). Having eaten all they could hold, they threw the flour into the sea to make the ship lighter.

39. Dawn came, but they didn't recognize the land. They spotted a cove with a beach, on which they planned to save the ship if at all possible. So they cut loose the anchors and left them in the sea. At the same time, they loosened the rudder yokes, hoisted the front sail to the wind and headed for the beach. But they struck an underwater reef and grounded the ship. The bow stuck so tight it wouldn't budge, while the stern was cracking up from the violence of the waves.

42. It was the guards' intention to kill the prisoners so as to keep any of them from swimming ashore and escaping. The captain, however, intent on saving Paul, turned thumbs down to their plan. He ordered all who could swim to jump off first and check out for land, and the rest to make it on planks or whatever they could get hold of from the ship. In this way everybody made it safely to shore.

28.

1. Later, when all were safe, we discovered that we were on the island of Malta. The local people were unusually friendly to us. Because it was cold and still raining they built a fire and invited us all in. Paul gathered quite a pile of wood, and as he was putting some on the fire, a poisonous snake, driven out by the heat, bit him on the hand. When the local people saw the critter still hanging on his hand, they said to each other, "Surely this guy is a murderer. Even though he survived the wreck, justice has finally caught up with him." Paul just shook the critter off into the fire and wasn't harmed a bit. They expected him to start swelling and to keel over dead any minute. After waiting a long while and noticing nothing unusual happening to him, they changed their tune. "He's a *god*!" they said.

7. The head man of the island, a fellow named Publius, owned some land in that area, and he put us up for three days and treated us royally. Publius' father was sick in bed with dysentery, and had a fever. Paul went to see him and prayed for him, then touched him with his hand and healed him. When this happened, all the rest of the people on the island who had sick ones brought them and had them healed. They even honored us with the very finest things they had, and when we left, they loaded us with everything we needed.

11. After spending three months there we set sail in an Alexandrian ship, the *Gemini,* which had wintered in the island. We arrived at Syracuse, spent three days there, and after a rather circuitous route, we made it to Rhegium. Next day the wind began blowing from the south, and two days later we reached Puteoli. We contacted some brothers there who invited us to spend the week with them.

15. And at last we made it to Rome! News about us had already reached the brothers there, and they came out and met us at Apius' store and Three Taverns. When Paul saw them he thanked God and perked up. In Rome itself Paul was permitted to live privately, but with a guard assigned to him.

(The scene changes, and Paul is once again our contemporary. He is in Washington to present his "case" to the Supreme Court.)

17. Three days after arriving, Paul called a meeting of some of the prominent whites, and when they had assembled he said to them, "Gentlemen and brothers, I am indeed a person who has in no way turned against my own people or their revered traditions. Yet I was jailed in Atlanta by the police, who examined me and wanted to release me, since I was guilty of violating no laws. But some hotheaded whites were gunning for me and I was forced to appeal to the Supreme Court, though I had no complaint against white people as such. So that's the reason I called you together—

to see and talk with you personally. For the sake of the white man's only hope I have this chain draped around my neck." They said to him, "Why, we have received no letters from the white people about you, nor have any of the brothers come here and reported or spoken any bad thing about you. But we are anxious to hear what you're thinking, because we do know that this offshoot belief is being attacked everywhere." They arranged another day with him, and a larger group came over to his house. He put his cards on the table, sharing his experiences in the God Movement and proving from the Scriptures the things about Jesus. The discussion lasted all day. Some were convinced by his arguments, but others couldn't take it. They got into an awful squabble and left. As they did, Paul took one final shot. "The Holy Spirit spoke so aptly through the prophet Isaiah when he said to your fathers:

'Go to these people and tell them,
"You strain your ears and never catch on,
You strain your eyes and never see the point."
For the hearts of these people are hard,
And their ears arc dull,
And their eyes are dim.
Otherwise, their eyes might see,
And their ears might hear,
And their hearts might melt,
And they might turn my way,
And I'll make them well.'

"So let this be absolutely clear to you: God has shared this victorious life with all whom you consider 'outsiders'. *They* will take it seriously."

30. Paul spent two whole years in his own rented house, and welcomed any who cared to visit him. All the while, with the utmost frankness and freedom, he was promoting the God Movement and teaching the lessons about the Lord Jesus Christ.

159